EUROCENTRISM

Samir Amin

EUROCENTRISM

TRANSLATED BY RUSSELL MOORE

MONTHLY REVIEW PRESS
NEW YORK

Copyright © 1989 by Monthly Review Press
All rights reserved

Originally published as *L'eurocentrisme: Critique d'une ideologie*
by Anthropos, Paris, France, © 1988 by Anthropos-Economica

Library of Congress Cataloging-in-Publication Data

Amin, Samir.
    [Eurocentrisme. English]
    Eurocentrism / Samir Amin.
        p.   cm.
    Translation of: L'eurocentrisme.
    Bibliography: p.
    ISBN 0-85345-785-9.   —   ISBN 0-85345-786-7 (pbk.)
    1. Europe—Economic conditions. 2. Europe—Social conditions.
3. Capitalism—Europe—History. I. Title.
HC240.A79513   1989
306.3—dc19
                                          88-36445
                                            CIP

Monthly Review Press
122 West 27th Street
New York, N.Y. 10001

Manufactured in the United States of America
10 9 8 7 6 5 4 3 2 1

Table of Contents

Preface

1. Eurocentrism is a culturalist phenomenon in the sense that it assumes the existence of irreducibly distinct cultural invariants that shape the historical paths of different peoples. Eurocentrism is therefore anti-universalist, since it is not interested in seeking possible general laws of human evolution. But it does present itself as universalist, for it claims that imitation of the Western model by all peoples is the only solution to the challenges of our time.

Eurocentrism is not the sum of Westerners' preconceptions, mistakes, and blunders with respect to other peoples. After all, these errors are no more serious than the corresponding presumptions that non-European peoples hold with respect to Westerners. Eurocentrism is thus not a banal ethnocentrism testifying simply to the limited horizons beyond which no people on this planet has yet truly been able to go. Eurocentrism is a specifically modern phenomenon, the roots of which go back only to the Renaissance, a phenomenon that did not flourish until the nineteenth century. In this sense, it constitutes one dimension of the culture and ideology of the modern capitalist world.

Eurocentrism is also not a social theory capable of providing the key to the interpretation of the questions that social theory proposes to elucidate. Eurocentrism is only a distortion—albeit a systematic and important one—from which the majority of dominant social theories and ideologies suffer. In other words, Eurocentrism is a paradigm which, like all paradigms, functions spontaneously, often in the gray areas of seemingly obvious facts and common sense. For this reason, it manifests itself in a variety of ways, as much in the expression of received ideas, popularized by the media, as in the erudite formulations of specialists in different areas of social science.

2. There are several ways of dealing with the subject.

The first would consist in treating the multiple manifestations of Eurocentrism, in order to expose the particular errors of each occurrence. Such a project would involve defining the distinct arenas in which Eurocentrism is manifested.

One investigation of this type would be a critique of the media version of the problems of the contemporary world. Such a project would involve the work of a research team, whose purpose it would be to analyze systematically major newspapers and television programs. To my knowledge, no project of this sort has been undertaken, although it undoubtedly deserves to be done. However, it is not the kind of project I propose to undertake here.

Other areas of the modern cultural edifice could be analyzed in the same fashion. Fortunately, there are a few works of note that have this type of analysis as their objective. Edward Said, for example, has written an excellent analysis of the Eurocentric distortion caused by Orientalism. Similarly, Martin Bernal has produced a penetrating study of "Hellenomania" and the construction of the myth of Greece as the "ancestor of the West." Moreover, a number of solid critiques of different aspects of racism can be found. I will obviously draw upon the conclusions of all of these important contributions.

The second possible way of dealing with the subject—and this will be my approach—proposes, from the outset, to go beyond these sectoral contributions to the critique of Eurocentrism and situate the phenomenon within the overall ideological construct of capitalism. It therefore becomes a question of determining precisely the particular functions of legitimation to which Eurocentrism responds. It also becomes necessary to show how these functions help to hide the nature of actually existing capitalism and to distort awareness of its contradictions.

This option has three consequences.

The first is that it makes it impossible to enter into the heart of the matter from the very first page of the book. The reader is therefore asked to show a little patience, something to which the quick readings of this day and age do not always predispose us. But if Eurocentrism is, as I claim, a recent mythological reconstruction of the history of Europe and the world, it is necessary to start by giving another vision of this history, at least for the period to which the mythical and real Europe belongs, from Greek antiquity through the Middle Ages. When Eurocentrism finally makes its appearance, in the second part of the book, it will be possible to see how it has developed in response to certain questions and in contrast to certain realities. At one point I had thought of inverting the order of presentation specifically for the satisfaction of the impatient reader's curiosity. But had the "composite sketch" of Eurocentrism—which will appear in due course in the text—been placed at the beginning, it would have seemed extremely hackneyed and, moreover, hardly convincing, since it reproduces the entire set of dominant ideas based upon so-called common sense.

The second consequence is that this analysis of Eurocentrism will by necessity raise the most difficult questions of social theory. From my point of view, however, the conceptual tools at our disposal are still entirely insufficient for the task. Social theory is fragmented, not only by the opposition—useful though it is—of various schools of thought, but also by the unequal development of disciplines at both ends of the spectrum of social science. There are perhaps economic theories of capitalism that approximately meet the criteria of science. But in the realm of the political (power) and of the cultural, there is hardly anything more than mere reflections. This severe assessment is of course far from being widely shared. Social thought is still encumbered by dogmatisms of every kind, concerned exclusively with restoring old structures and, by means of dubious acrobatics, reproducing the same old answers to new questions. Graver still is the fact that, in response to the disillusionment and crisis of our time, the best-selling works of social theory are based on neoliberal theology, whose answer to everything—facile though it might be—has the advantage, nevertheless, of reassuring and legitimating preconceptions, a characteristic which undoubtedly accounts for its success.

The third consequence is that the paradigm of Eurocentrism—like any paradigm—cannot be overturned by a simple internal critique of its weaknesses. It answers real questions, even if we may think that it does so in an erroneous fashion. It is therefore necessary to replace it with correct positive responses—even knowing that the conceptual tools at our disposal remain feeble. It is therefore a question of a long, arduous, and complex task of reconstruction, and I do not aim to produce a global theory in these pages. Nevertheless, I shall advance some of the elements of this reconstruction, elements which seem to me indispensable.

3. The outline of the work follows from the preceding observations.

The critique of Eurocentrism proposed in this work is based on a hypothesis concerning the theory of culture, since Eurocentrism is a cultural phenomenon. In the first part, I will develop, on the basis of this hypothesis, the idea that precapitalist Europe in its cultural dimensions is part of a broader "peripheral tributary" ideological construct. In the second part, I will show the ambiguities of the new capitalist culture developed from the Renaissance onward. On the one hand, the new culture breaks with its tributary past (a break which gives it its progressive dimension and feeds its universalist ambition). But on the other, it reconstructs itself on mythical foundations, whose function is to blur the extent of this rupture with the past through an affirmation of a nonexistent historical continuity. This false continuity constitutes the core of the Eurocentric dimension of capitalist culture, the very dimension which undermines its intended universalist scope.

4. This project for a critique of Eurocentrism is meaningless if it is not acknowledged from the start that capitalism has created a real objective need for universalism, both at the level of scientific explanation of the evolution of human societies (in particular, the explanation of different courses of evolution by means of a single conceptual system) and the elaboration of a program for the future which addresses humanity as a whole.

However, this proposition is not evident to everyone; there are three distinct attitudes toward the subject.

For some—a group more numerous than is often thought— there is no need for universalism. The "right to be different" (apartheid?) and the culturalist praise of provincialisms do away with the problem. This position implies accepting as natural and insurmountable the breakdown of theory into distinct, multiple areas and the triumph of pragmatism in each.

For others, who represent the dominant Eurocentric current, the answer to the question exists: Europe has already discovered it. This group's slogan is thus: "Imitate the West, the best of all possible worlds." The liberal utopia and its miracle prescription (marketplace plus democracy) are only the poor version currently in fashion of this permanent, dominant vision in the West. Its success with the media does not confer upon it any scientific value; but such success does testify to the profundity of the crisis of Western thought. For this Eurocentric vision, based upon a stubborn refusal to comprehend the nature of actually existing capitalism, is perhaps neither desirable nor desired by the victims of this system. It is, perhaps, even impossible without calling into question the foundations of the very system that it defends.

I will therefore place myself in the third camp, with those who think that we are at a serious impasse and that it is consequently worth the trouble to discuss its nature.

5. The choice of the term "Eurocentrism" may itself be open to discussion. If by it we mean to refer to an essential dimension of the ideology of capitalism, its manifestations would be characteristic of the common dominant attitudes of all of the societies in the developed capitalist world, the center of the world capitalist system. Today, this center is composed of Western Europe, North America, Japan, and a few other states (Australia, New Zealand, Israel), with Latin America and the Antilles, Africa, and noncommunist Asia (excepting Japan) constituting the peripheral states. The very center of these centers is North America; Japan is neither Western, nor Christian; Latin America is to a large

extent a product of the expansion of Europe. The socialist world itself has a history that it cannot entirely erase (despite the slogan, "Let us make a clean slate of the past"): It is European in Europe, Asiatic in Asia.

On the other hand, at least until the end of the Second World War, each European country's enemy was another European country, and chauvinistic nationalisms could overshadow the feeling of a common European identity. Hitler went so far as to apply to non-German Europeans the general European racism toward other peoples. It is only since 1945 that a common European consciousness has seemed to be gaining the upper hand over local, provincial, and national sentiments.

However, even if the term "Occidentalocentrism" were substituted for "Eurocentrism" (using the common definition of the term "the West"), it would not be possible to provide a better account of such cases as Latin America and Japan, even if the importance of the European origin of capitalist culture were denied. All things considered, "Eurocentrism" says quite well exactly what it means to say.

This subject is not new to me. For thirty years, all of my efforts have been dedicated to seeking a way to strengthen the universalist dimension of historical materialism; my thesis concerning unequal development is an expression of the results of these efforts. Thus the reader who has already read some of my works will find him or herself on familiar ground. I have nevertheless conceived this book as a self-contained whole.

Introduction

1. Capitalism has produced a decisive break in world history, whose reach extends beyond the simple, albeit prodigious, progress of productive forces it has achieved. Indeed, capitalism has overturned the structure of relationships among different aspects of social life (economic organization, political order, the content and function of ideologies) and has refashioned them on qualitatively new foundations.

  In all earlier social systems, the economic phenomenon is transparent. By this I mean that the destination of that which is produced is immediately visible: The major part of production is directly consumed by the producers themselves. Moreover, the surplus levied by the ruling classes assumes the form of rents and various fees, often in kind or in labor: in short, the form of a tribute, whose deduction does not escape the immediate perception of those who shoulder its burden. Market exchange and wage labor are, of course, not entirely absent, but they remain limited in their range and marginal in their social and economic scope. Under these conditions, the economic phenomenon remains too simple—that is to say, too immediately apprehensible—to give rise to a "science of economics" elucidating its mysteries. Science becomes necessary to explain an area of reality only when laws that are not directly visible operate behind the immediately apparent facts: that is, only when this

1

area has become opaque due to the laws which govern its movement.

The reproduction of precapitalist social systems rests upon the stability of power (which is the basic concept defining the domain of the political) and of an ideology that endows it with legitimacy. In other words, politico-ideological authority (the "superstructure") is dominant at this point. The mystery that must be elucidated in order to understand the genesis, reproduction, and evolution of these societies and of the contradictions within which they operate is to be found in the area of the politico-ideological, not in the realm of the economic. In other words, what we need here is a genuine theory of culture, capable of accounting for the functioning of social power.

Capitalism inverts the order of the relationships between the realm of the economic and the politico-ideological superstructure. The newly developed economic life is no longer transparent, due to the generalization of the market: Not only does the near totality of the social product take the form of goods whose final destination escapes the control of the producer, but the labor force itself, in its predominant wage-earning form, becomes commodified. For this reason, the levy on the surplus takes the form of profits, profits which are always aleatory (they only materialize under certain conditions in the manufacturing of the product), while the exploitation of labor is obscured by the legal equivalence which defines the buying and selling of the wage-labor force. Henceforth, economic laws operate in the reproduction of the system as hidden objective forces. This mystified economic authority, now dominant, constitutes a domain which hereafter invites scientific analysis. And the content as well as the social function of power and ideology acquire, in this reproduction, new characteristics which are qualitatively different from those by which social power was defined in earlier societies. Any theory of culture must take into consideration this new, inverted relation under capitalism of the economic and the politico-ideological.

There is therefore no symmetry between these two domains in precapitalist and capitalist societies. In this context, the vulgar Marxist doctrine according to which power is the expression of class domination and ideology the articulation of the requirements for the exercise of that domination, is of little use for understanding reality. Although true at the highest level of abstraction, this theory obscures the qualitative difference discussed above, namely the reversal of relations between the two instances, economic and politico-ideological. This doctrine cannot therefore constitute a point of departure for a theory of the political and the cultural.

Having chosen to underscore this crucial reversal from the beginning, I have thought it necessary to give the same name to all precapitalist systems. To refer to them all as incidences of the tributary mode of production seems to me most suitable, because the term emphasizes the transparent character of economic exploitation in these societies. Let me observe that I am only considering here the advanced precapitalist societies (in which classes and state are clearly crystallized), and not the societies of the earlier stage (in which classes and state are not yet definitively crystallized), which I refer to as examples of the communal mode of production. Obviously, each tributary society has its own specific characteristics, which taken together present an almost infinite variety. But, beyond this variety, tributary societies form a single family characterized by the same arrangement of economy and superstructure.

2. Our instruments for the theoretical analysis of social reality, however, remain rather imperfect.

This social reality, considered in its totality, has three dimensions: economic, political, and cultural. The economy probably constitutes the best-known dimension of social reality. Bourgeois economics has forged instruments for its analysis and, with a greater or lesser degree of success, for the management of capitalist society. Historical materialism has gone further in depth and often successfully casts light upon the nature and scope of the social struggles that underlie economic choices.

The domain of power and the political is considerably less well known, and the eclecticism of the various theories that have been proposed reflects the feeble mastery of this area of reality. American functionalist political economy, as well as its older or more recent component parts (geopolitics, systems analysis, etc.), even if sometimes effective in immediate action, share a conceptual poverty that negates any pretense they may have of holding the status of critical theory. Here as well historical materialism has proposed a hypothesis with respect to the organic relationship between material base and political superstructure which, if interpreted in a nondogmatic manner, can be useful. Nevertheless, Marxism has not conceptualized the question of power and the political (the modes of domination) in the same way that it has the economic (the modes of production). The proposals that have been made in this direction, for example by Freudian Marxism, though undoubtedly interesting for having called attention to certain neglected aspects of the problem, have not yet produced a fruitful general conceptual system. The field of the political remains therefore practically fallow.

It is not by chance that "The Fetishism of Commodities" is the title of the first chapter of Book One of *Das Kapital*. Marx intends to reveal the secret of capitalist society, the logic that causes it to present itself as being directly under the control of the economy, which occupies the center stage of society and, in its unfolding, determines the other dimensions of society, which appear to have to adjust themselves to its demands. Economic alienation thus constitutes the essential content of the ideology of capitalism. Precapitalist class societies are, by contrast, controlled by the political, to whose constraints the other aspects of social reality— among others, economic life—seem to have to submit. If, therefore, one were to write the theory of the tributary mode of production, the title of the work would have to be *Power,* instead of *Capital* for the capitalist mode, and the title of the first chapter "The Fetishism of Power" instead of "The Fetishism of Commodities."

But such a work has not been written, nor anything analogous to the precise analysis which, like clockwork, describes the economic functioning of capitalism. Marxism has not produced a theory of the political for precapitalist society (or, indeed, a general theory of the political) as it has produced a theory of the capitalist economy. At best, there have been concrete analyses of the functioning of the political/economic relationship in particular capitalist societies (in Marx's political writings, for example, especially those devoted to the vicissitudes of France), analyses that highlight the degree of autonomy the political enjoys in these societies and the conflict that can arise as a result between the logic of power and the logic of capitalist administration.

As for the cultural dimension, it remains mysterious and unknown; empirical observation of cultural phenomena (religion, for example) has not produced, up until now, anything more than some intuitive essays. This is why the treatment of the cultural dimensions of history remains imbued with traces of culturalism, meaning a tendency to treat cultural characteristics as transhistorical constants. Thus there is no generally accepted definition of the domain of culture, for the definition depends on the underlying theory of social dynamics that one adopts. For this reason, depending on whether the goal is to discover the common dynamics of the social evolution of all peoples, or whether, on the contrary, this search is abandoned, the emphasis will be placed either on the characteristics that are analogous and common to the various, apparently different cultures, or on the particular and the specific.

Finally, the structural relationship of these three dimensions of the social reality remain almost unknown, apart from *a posteriori* explanations and highly general abstractions (like the affirmation of determination "in the last instance" by the material base). As long as there have not been any important advances in this domain, all discussion will remain hindered by emotional reactions and romantic visions.

What I propose in this work is not to develop a theory of power and culture capable of filling in the aforementioned gaps; rather, I have only the ambition of contributing to the construction of a paradigm freed from culturalist distortion.

3. To recognize, from the outset, the diversity of human cultures is only to state a truism which can obscure the conceptual difficulty of grasping the nature and scope of the problem. For where are the boundaries in space and time of a particular culture? On what bases may its singularity be defined? For example, is it possible to speak today of a European culture encompassing the West as a whole, in spite of linguistic differences? If the answer is yes, should that European culture also include Eastern Europe, in spite of its different political and

social regime; Latin America, in spite of its underdevelopment; or Japan, in spite of its non-European historical roots? Is it possible to speak of a single culture encompassing the Arab or Arab-Islamic world, or sub-Saharan Africa, or India? Or must these broad categories be abandoned in favor of observing the specificities of their component subgroups? But then where does one draw the line in the unending divisions and subdivisions of provincial singularity? And what is the pertinence of the differences observed; what capacity do they have for explaining social change?

On the other hand, it is possible to emphasize the common characteristics shared by different societies at the same general stage of development and, from this base, define a communal and a tributary culture, just as I have identified a communal and a tributary stage. It is then possible to situate specific components within the framework of these general categories. My hypothesis is that all tributary cultures are based upon the preeminence of the metaphysical aspiration, by which I mean the search for absolute truth. This religious or quasi-religious character of the dominant ideology of tributary societies responds to an essential requirement of the social reproduction of these societies. By contrast, the culture of capitalism is founded upon the renunciation of this metaphysical aspiration in favor of a search for partial truths. Simultaneously, the ideology peculiar to the new society acquires a dominant economistic content necessary for the social reproduction of capitalism. By *economism,* I mean that economic laws are considered as objective laws imposing themselves on society as forces of nature, or, in other words, as forces outside of the social relationships peculiar to capitalism.

This shifting of the center of gravity of the dominant ideology from the sphere of what I call metaphysical alienation (or religious alienation, or even alienation from nature) to the sphere of market alienation (peculiar to economism) constitutes the core of the cultural revolution that ensures the passage from the tributary period to the Age of Capital. This revolution certainly does not suppress metaphysical aspirations or religion. But it adapts religion to the new world, relying on religion's inherent flexibility, and represses it outside of the field of legitimation of the social order. The cultural revolution of capitalism always includes, as a result, a particular side effect: It is also a religious revolution, a revolution in the interpretation of religion.

But that is not all. In tributary societies, as in capitalist ones, I propose to distinguish the completed central forms from the uncompleted peripheral ones. The criterion that defines the terms of the center/periphery contrast, one of the keys of the analysis, is derived from the dominant sphere characteristic of each of the two successive social systems. In capitalism the center/periphery contrast is defined therefore in economic terms: at one end are the dominating, completed capitalist societies; at the other end are the dominated, unfinished, backward capitalist societies. Economic domination (and its complement, economic dependence) is the product of the worldwide expansion of actually existing capitalism. On the other hand, the central and/or peripheral forms of tributary society are not defined in economic terms—even less so in terms of economic domination and dependence—but are characterized by the finished and/or unfinished degree of state formation and ideological expression. Thus feudal European society seems for this reason to exemplify the peripheral form of the tributary mode. The disappearance of the centralized state in feudal Europe in favor of a dispersal of social power is the most striking manifestation of this peripheral character. At the level of ideology and culture, the contrast between central tributary societies and peripheral tributary ones is marked by significant differences.

History seems to show that peripheral tributary societies experienced less difficulty than central tributary societies in advancing in the capitalist direction. This greater flexibility of the less advanced societies seems to us to be central to the theory of unequal development.

The first part of the text that follows treats these propositions concerning tributary culture in its central and peripheral forms. These reflections are developed from the starting point of a comparison between Christian feudal Europe and the Arab-Islamic East. The general validity of the hypothesis will be demonstrated by the fruitfulness of extending it into other fields, notably the Chinese and Confucian world.

4. In imposing itself on a worldwide scale, capitalism has created a twofold demand for universalism: first, at the level of the scientific analysis of society, that is to say, at the level of the discovery of universal laws that govern all societies; and second, at the level of the elaboration of a universal human project allowing the supercession of the historical limits of capitalism itself.

What are these historical limits? The answer depends on the understanding that one has of capitalism itself. Two stances are possible. One can focus on that which defines capitalism at its highest level of abstraction—namely, the capital/labor contradiction—and define the historical limits of capitalist society by the boundaries imposed by its characteristic economic laws. This point of view inevitably inspires a "stagist" vision of the evolution of society: the backward (peripheral) capitalist societies must "catch up" with the advanced societies before they can, in turn, confront the challenge of possibly (or even perhaps necessarily) bypassing their limits. On the other hand, one may place more emphasis in one's analysis on what I propose to call "actually existing capitalism," by which I mean a system that, in its actual worldwide expansion, has generated a center/periphery polarization impossible to overcome within the framework of capitalism itself. From this perspective, another characteristic of unequal development is revealed: namely, that the calling into question of the capitalist mode of social organization is more deeply felt as an objective necessity at the periphery of the system than at its center.

Does the ideology produced by capitalism in these conditions allow a response to these challenges? Or rather, in its real historical development, has it only produced a truncated universalism incapable of resolving the problems engendered by its own expansion? What are the elements from which one might begin to conceptualize a truly universalist cultural project? Such are the questions that I propose to examine in the second part of the text.

5. The European culture that conquered the world fashioned itself in the course of a history that unfolded in two distinct time periods. Up until the Renaissance, Europe belonged to a regional tributary system that included Europeans and Arabs, Christians and Moslems. But the greater part of Europe at that time was located at the periphery of this regional system, whose center was situated around the eastern end of the Mediterranean basin. This Mediterranean system prefigures to some extent the subsequent capitalist world system. From the Renaissance on, the capitalist world system shifts its center toward the shores of the Atlantic, while the Mediterranean region becomes, in turn, the periphery. The new European culture reconstructs itself around a myth that

creates an opposition between an alleged European geographical continuity and the world to the south of the Mediterranean, which forms the new center/periphery boundary. The whole of Eurocentrism lies in this mythic construct.

PART ONE

Central and Peripheral Tributary Cultures

I.

The Formation of Tributary Ideology in the Mediterranean Region

1. The Ancient World

The Age of Antiquity is in fact a plural reality; it is therefore more appropriate to speak of the *Ages* of Antiquity. On a map of the region, those zones in which there appears a marked development of the productive forces, allowing for the clear crystallization of the state and social classes, are isolated from each other. In this manner, over the course of a few millennia, Egypt, Mesopotamia, and then Persia and Greece are constituted in relative isolation (an isolation which is more marked in the most ancient periods and the most precocious civilizations of the Nile and Mesopotamian valleys, and less so for Greece, which is formed in the course of the last millennium preceding the Christian era). These civilizations are islands in the ocean of the still widespread, dominant barbarity: that is to say, in a world still characterized by the predominance of the communal mode of production (as opposed to the tributary mode that typifies the civilizations in question).

Each of these more developed civilizations has its own structure and particular characteristics. The search for a common denominator at the level of their systems of ideas could therefore

15

seem to be virtually impossible. Nevertheless, thanks to the distance of time, it is possible to isolate some common traits belonging to the long period of pre-Hellenistic history, traits which contrast with the characteristics of the thought and ideological formation of the medieval era.

Firstly, these traits are common to all of the peoples in the region under examination, whether they be barbarian (Celts, Germans, Slavs, Berbers, Arabs) or civilized (Egyptians, Assyrians and Babylonians, Phoenicians, Hittites, Persians, Greeks). In other words, there is no marked qualitative distance, at this level, between the modes of thought of communal societies and those of tributary societies during their first stage. There are, of course, more or less significant quantitative differences, and even some partial qualitative breakthroughs, to which I will return later.

Secondly, there exists at this stage an empirical scientific practice, but hardly any scientific thinking. Empirical practice—in the areas of agriculture, animal husbandry, navigation, construction, and handicrafts (textiles, pottery, metallurgy)—is as old as humanity itself. Of course this activity is in direct relationship with the development of the productive forces, of which it is both cause and effect as part of an intimate dialectical relationship. But for quite a long period, these practices do not necessarily imply any abstract scientific systemization. Obviously, the practice of borrowing between societies is also current practice at the time.

Thirdly, the widespread practice of elaborating mythologies dealing with the formation of the universe, humankind (and especially the people to whom the mythology speaks), and the social order (division of labor, organization of the family, various powers, etc.) remains marked by the territory of its origin. There is no claim to universality. Neither is there any coherent systemat-

ic relationship between the mythologies in question and empirical practice. The juxtaposition of distinct forms of knowledge—
those I would term scientific because they are developed through
empirical practice, and those that I would refrain from designating in this way—characterizes the mode of thought of the ancient
world. However developed any one civilization may be with
respect to others (as defined by a higher level of productive
forces, the development of the state and writing), these mythologies are equivalent: the myth of Osiris and Isis; Greek, Celtic or
other myths (and one might add, by extrapolation, African or
Indo-American mythologies); the Bible. No hierarchical classification of them makes any sense at all. Moreover, the fact that
certain of these mythologies (such as the Bible) have survived
from antiquity and have been integrated into medieval thought
and ideology does not mean that they have any superior intrinsic
value.

Fourthly, social thought—which obviously exists in these
societies—has neither scientific pretensions, nor even any awareness that society might be an object of a reflection that, in my
opinion, could be qualified as being scientific. Social thought
justifies the existing order, understood as eternal, and that is all.
Any idea of progress is excluded.

Nevertheless, in spite of the general nature of these shared
traits, it is also necessary to mention the breakthroughs that, from
time to time, prefigure later ideological constructs and modes of
thought. I will mention four of these.

Before any other people, the Egyptians introduce the concept
of eternal life and immanent moral justice, opening the way for
humanist universalism. Everywhere else, including pre-Hellenistic
Greece, the status of what one will later call the "soul" and the
fate of the human being after death remain uncertain and vague.

The "spirits of the dead" are feared for their malevolent power of intervention in the world of the living. In this light, one can clearly see the degree of progress represented by the invention of the "immortal soul" and the idea of "individual rewards and punishment," founded on a universal morality that scrutinizes the motives and intentions of human actions. It matters little that, nowadays, immortality and divine justice are only considered acts of religious faith, and no longer as "points of fact," or much less as "scientifically established" facts. The universalist moral break-through of the Egyptians is the keystone of subsequent human thought. It takes several centuries, however, before this Egyptian invention becomes a commonplace. We will see an example of this later on with respect to the debates between Christianity and Islam concerning Hell and Paradise, individual responsibility and determinism, the foundations of belief.

Egypt's real contribution lies in this breakthrough and not, as is so often claimed, in the invention of monotheism by Akhenaten. For the universalist concept of immanent justice is compatible with all forms of religious belief, pantheist as well as enlightened, including, for example, Hindu religious thought in all its rich-ness. On the other hand, the concept of monotheism, which will impose itself in this region of the world (and nowhere else), perhaps in part because it responds to a paralogical simplifica-tion, is in fact the product of the absolutism of power in Egyptian civilization, more advanced than any other tributary society. It is therefore not surprising that this principle comes to constitute one of the keystones of the tributary ideological construct of the region during medieval times. But it must be pointed out that the exportation of the monotheist principle to peoples less advanced along the road of tributary development has not proven fruitful. Judaism was founded, as is well known, upon this borrowing.

This has not prevented it from remaining primitive in its essential foundations: Judaism has remained a religion without any universalist aspiration (it is exclusively that of the "chosen people"), marked by a mythological attachment (the Bible), and, to some extent, lacking a concept of immanent justice as developed as that of the Egyptians. Later on, Judaism, benefiting from the advances made first by Hellenism (in the time of Philo),* then by Islam (notably in Andalusia), and later by Christian and, finally, modern capitalist Europe, reinterpreted its beliefs in a less restricted sense.

Greece produced an explosion in the fields of scientific abstraction, the philosophy of nature, and social thought whose adoption only occurred later, during the medieval period. Empiricist practice—as old as humankind itself—finally came to pose questions of the human mind that required a more systematic effort of abstraction. The birth of astronomy, calculus, and mathematics represents the first wave of this practice, followed by the fields of chemistry and physics. After Mesopotamian astronomy and Egyptian calculus, Greek mathematics constitutes a qualitative leap forward which, enriched by the Arabs, will only be surpassed in modern times. Ahead of the needs of empiricist practice, mathematics develops by turning inward and nurturing itself upon its own substance, and therefore inspires the first chapters of logic. But precisely because its relationship with the enrichment of empiricist practice still remains a tenuous one, its drift toward the realm of mythic relationships is difficult to avoid.

The joining of the new mathematics and the new logic on the

---

*The philosopher Philo (30 B.C.–45 A.D.) was a key mediating figure between Hellenism and both Christianity and Neoplatonism. (Ed.)

one hand, and empiricist practice on the other, inspired the development of a philosophy of nature with the potential vocation of replacing mythologies of creation. Here I do mean philosophy of nature and not metaphysics. The former characterizes the breakthrough of pre-Hellenistic Greek philosophy; the latter becomes synonymous with philosophy during the medieval period before losing its monopoly once again in modern times. The philosophy of nature is an attempt at abstraction that makes it possible to grant coherence to the whole of knowledge through the search for the "general laws" which govern nature. In this sense, as Marx and Engels keenly felt, the philosophy of nature is essentially materialist: It seeks to explain the world by the world itself. Undoubtedly, this search for general laws remains marked by the limits of relative, real knowledge; the progress from classical mechanistic philosophy to the modern philosophies of nature is only quantitative.

The key breakthrough in the philosophy of nature posits the existence of an eternal universe in permanent motion (from Heraclitus, 540–480 B.C., until the atomism of Democritus, 460–364 B.C.). The reconciliation of this principle with medieval religious beliefs (Hellenistic, Christian, and Islamic) does not take place without some difficulty, as we shall see later on.

Greek social thought does not really produce any truly remarkable breakthroughs. In fact, in the area of social thought, it will not be until the appearance of ibn-Khaldun that one may begin to speak of a scientific concept of history. Concurrently, Greece borrowed numerous things from other cultures, most notably Egypt. Its technological borrowings were decisive in the flourishing of its civilization. Egypt's moral universalism, however, made no inroads until the time of Socrates and Plato.

The breakthroughs that take place in these various domains

remain unintegrated into a global vision and without any strong links between them. Hellenistic, and later Christian and Islamic, metaphysics will accomplish this synthesis, of which only a few scattered elements are available at the end of the golden age of Classical Greece.

I will not put on the same level the breakthroughs made in Mesopotamia or those transported from India by way of the Persians. I only mention them because they will find their place in the subsequent medieval construct.

Mesopotamia furnished, first of all, an astronomy that— however descriptive it might have been—was nonetheless largely accurate and produced as a result of rigorous observation. This heritage, rediscovered during the Hellenistic period, was developed later on, notably by the Arabs and then of course in modern times. But this is not where the essential point of my interest lies. The Chaldeans also produced a general mythology of the universe in which the stars are situated with respect to—and above—what was later called the sublunary world. From this mythology, vaguely linked to their scientific astronomy, they derived an astrology. It is this same mythology and the astrology derived from it which subsequently find their place in the general medieval construct.

It is not my purpose here to examine the evolution of thought to the east of the Indus, its scientific contributions, its mythologies, or the elaboration of its pantheism, its morality, and its global conception of life. But it must be noted that here as well a breakthrough in the direction of the conceptualization of the "soul" was also produced, and, it seems, rather early on. This development was intimately linked to a specific philosophy that invites the individual to experience detachment from the constraints of nature in order to realize the plenitude of knowledge and happiness. Its call to asceticism as a means of liberation crossed the borders of India and entered the East and then the West from the earliest stages of the formation of medieval civilization. From the Hellenistic period onward, the call to asceticism came to penetrate Eastern and Western thought and to flourish in the later forms of Christianity and Islam. For this reason, and because this conception will later be integrated into the medieval construct, it is necessary to mention it here.

In conclusion, what takes place in this area as a whole over this long period of time is in fact the slow constitution of the tributary ideological construct, that is to say, the construction of an overall worldview (in the sense of *Weltanschauung*) that meets the fundamental requirements for the reproduction of the tributary mode, irrespective of its specific forms.

The transparency of the relationships of exploitation in these societies demands that the ideological play a predominant role and be regarded as sacred. Earlier communal relationships did not require such coherence from their ideological constructs; that is why the barbarian forms of ancient thought juxtapose empiricism, mythology of nature, and mythology of society without any problem. The passage to the tributary form demands a greater degree of coherence and the integration of the elements of abstract knowledge into a global metaphysics. It is not until the modern age that the mystification of social relationships, peculiar to capitalism, can overthrow the domination of this sacred ideology and replace it with the rule of the economic. Simultaneously, this new economic rule, which will only be desecrated with the abolition of capitalism, creates the conditions that allow for the renunciation of the aspiration for a universalizing metaphysics.

In the course of the construction of tributary ideology, which comes to flourish throughout the medieval period, Ancient Egypt holds a particular place. For the core of this ideology is already present in the accomplishments of Egypt, which passes from a moral science with a potential for universalism that functions as the justifier of the social order, to an all-encompassing metaphysics that furnishes Hellenism, and later Islam and Christianity, with their point of departure, as the thinkers of the period themselves recognized.

Medieval scholastic metaphysics in its four successive forms—Hellenistic, Eastern Christian, Islamic, and Western Christian—constitutes the ideology *par excellence* of the tributary mode of production. Without broaching the forms assumed by this tributary ideology in the other regions of the world (China, India, etc.), it is possible to assert that, beyond the originality of their specific manifestations, these forms respond to the fundamental need of tributary reproduction.

By contrast, the ideology of the communal modes, spanning the long transition from primitive communism to the development of class and state society, is of a qualitatively different nature. Here the essential content of the ideology is in a strict relationship of extreme dependency on nature (a result of the weak development of the productive forces) and the still embryonic character of the classes and the state. Communal ideology is an ideology of nature: The human being and society are assimilated to other expressions of nature (animals, plants, environment), and are conceptualized as such. The predominance of kinship relations, in both the organization of social reality and the conception of relationships to nature, undergoes an evolution in both form and content from primitive communism to the communal societies, an evolution which lies outside of the scope of the analysis presented here. The Age of Antiquity constitutes the last chapter of this evolution, a kind of transition to the tributary stage. Hence the "primitive" aspects of this Age of Antiquity, seen in the vestiges of communal ideology. There should be no cause for amazement that the breakthroughs in the direction of the tributary ideological construct are realized in Egypt, which is already a completed tributary society on the social level.

The tableau of the thought of the ancient East proposed here emphasizes the singularity of the contribution made by each of the regions in this part of the world. This singularity does not exclude the kinship of these diverse cultures, which all belong to the same stage of general societal development. Just as the societies of the region are capable of exchanging products and techniques on the material level, so they undertake equally intense exchanges at the level of ideas. Obviously the singularity of the particular contributions noted here only becomes meaningful with respect to the subsequent construction of medieval metaphysics, which integrates these contributions in its general synthesis. In this ongoing process of construction, one cannot establish any opposition between Greek thought (in order to make it the ancestor of modern European thought) and "Oriental" thought (from which Greece would be excluded). The opposition Greece = the West / Egypt, Mesopotamia, Persia = the East is itself a later artificial construct of Eurocentrism. For the boundary in the region separates the backward North African and European West from the advanced East; and the geographic unities constituting Europe, Africa, and Asia have no importance on the level of the history of civilization, even if Eurocentrism in its reading of the past has projected onto the past the modern North-South line of demarcation passing through the Mediterranean.

2. General Characteristics of Medieval Ideology

The constitution of Alexander's empire opens a genuinely new era for the entire region, for it brings to a definitive end the relative isolation of its different peoples and opens up the prospect for their possible subsequent unification. Until that time, attempts at conquest had only been sporadic, short-lived adventures without any lasting effect. Egypt only conquered the borderlands of contiguous western Asia in order to strengthen its defenses against barbaric nomads. The Assyrian and Persian expansions were neither strong enough nor durable enough to accomplish what Hellenism would realize: the unification of the ruling classes and of culture.

Hellenistic unification is, first of all, limited to the Orient: from Greece and Egypt to Persia. But it comprises all of the civilizations of the region as well as the more or less barbarian enclaves that, though progressively weakened, had separated these civilized groups from each other. The subsequent formation of the Roman Empire did not contribute anything really new to the Hellenistic Orient, though it did transport elements of its civilization and culture back to the Italian, Celtic, Berber, and finally Germanic West.

This unification brought to a definitive end the quasi-absolute independence of the states and peoples of the vast region that later became the Euro-Arab world (or the Euro-Christian and Arab-Islamic worlds). Not in the sense that any single state or a few "great states" have dominated the region as a whole at any one given time. Rather political fragmentation—pushed to the limit during the time of European feudalism—or, more modestly stated, the break-up of empire, on the basis of which the modern European and Arab states were later formed, no longer precluded the possibility of belonging to a single unique area of culture, just as a density of exchanges on the material and spiritual level became permanent.

One world or two? For a millennium, the split is vertical and separates the more civilized Orient (marked by the founding of the Byzantine Empire) from the semi-barbarous West. During the millennium and a half that follows, the split shifts so as to separate the North—Christian Europe—from the South—the Arab, Turkish, and Persian Islamic world. In Europe, civilization gradually wins over the peoples of the North and East; to the south of the Mediterranean, Islamic culture gains ground in the Maghreb. Christianity and Islam are thus both heirs of Hellenism and remain, for this reason, twin siblings, even if they have been, at certain moments, relentless adversaries. It is probably only in modern times—when Europe, from the Renaissance onward, takes off on the road toward capitalism—that the Mediterranean boundary line forms between what will crystallize as the center and periphery of the new worldwide and all-inclusive system. From then on, the Euro-Islamic medieval world ceases to exist as a unique cultural area and splits into two worlds that are henceforward unequal: Europe no longer has anything to learn from the peoples to the south of the Mediterranean. As far as Egypt is concerned, Hellenistic unification puts an end to its earlier decisive role in the history of the region. Egypt is henceforth a province in a larger whole. The country is subjected to a relatively subordinate status (in the Byzantine Empire, during the first three centuries following the Hegira, and then during the seventeenth and eighteenth century Ottoman Empire), until it becomes the center of gravity of the region (during the Ptolemaic, Fatimite, and Mameluke periods, and later with the renascent Arab nation of the beginning of the nineteenth century). But

Egypt is no longer confined in the "splendid isolation" that radiated across three millennia of its ancient history.

Now this Hellenistic, then Christian and/or Arab-Islamic unification had some profound and lasting effects. First of all, at the level of the development of productive forces, this unification obviously facilitated the transfer of technical advances and scientific knowledge and did so notably by extending them among peoples who are still barbaric. Moreover, this transfer occurred at the level of social organization, political forms, linguistic, cultural and religious communications, and philosophical ideas. The sense of relativity produced by the intensity of these relationships created a new kind of malaise, in the face of which local religions gradually lost their hold. The syncretisms of the Hellenistic period thus prepare the ground for Christianity and Islam, the bearers and sowers of a new universalist message. The social crisis which so frequently is used to describe the end of the Roman Empire, rather than being a crisis in the mode of production (although it is also in part the crisis of the predominant slave system in Greece and in Rome), was above all the product of this general and complex questioning.

The medieval construct unfolds in three time periods: a first Hellenistic period (approximately three centuries B.C.); a second Christian period, first appearing in the East (from the first until the seventh century of the Christian era) and then, much later, in the West (starting in the twelfth century); and finally, a third Islamic period (from the seventh until the twelfth century). The core of this construct goes back, as we will see, to the Hellenistic period. Neoplatonism serves as the base for the constitution of the first Christian scholasticism (in the East), an Islamic scholasticism, and finally the second Christian scholasticism (in the West), this last form being greatly imbued with Islamic thought. Undoubtedly each of these periods has its own specific traits and its particular interpretations; but, in my opinion, the common characteristics far outweigh the differences. In fact, it is their common, shared opposition to the characteristics of ancient thought that makes it possible to speak of medieval thought in a general manner.

The fundamental characteristic of medieval thought is the triumph of metaphysics, henceforth considered synonymous with philosophy (or wisdom). This trait is to be found in Hellenism, as well as in subsequent Islamic and Christian scholasticism.

Metaphysics proposes to discover the ultimate principle governing the universe in its totality: namely, "absolute truth." It is not interested in "partial truths" established by means of particular sciences; or, more precisely, it is only interested in them to the extent that these partial truths can contribute to the discovery of the final principles governing the universe. Of course, every religion is by definition a form of metaphysics. But the inverse is not true. For religion is founded on sacred texts, whereas one may conceive of a secular metaphysics, free from all revelation. Indeed, as the Islamic and Christian scholastics note, metaphysics claims to discover absolute truth solely through the use of deductive reason, whereas religion possesses in this regard revealed texts. The entire enterprise of Islamic and Christian metaphysics will consist in seeking to establish that there is no conflict between the use of this deductive reason and the content of the revealed texts (on the condition, of course, that one interprets these texts correctly).

The triumph of the metaphysical preoccupation entails, obviously, grave consequences for thought. Does this preoccupation devalue specialized scientific research and technical empiricism?

In theory, it does. Still, it is necessary to qualify the statement. For Hellenistic civilization, to take an example, was marked by important progress in astronomy and medicine, just as Arab-Islamic civilization was; the latter pushed, moreover, even farther ahead in the fields of mathematics and chemistry. Finally, particular scientific fields of inquiry satisfactorily resisted the triumph of the metaphysicians; indeed, they could even be stimulated by the hope of enriching metaphysics through scientific discoveries. As for empiricism, which has been until very recently practically the sole foundation for the progress of the productive forces, it goes quietly along without worrying about intellectual powers that by and large hold it in contempt.

What the new metaphysics—which will crystallize into scholasticism—calls human reason is, in fact, exclusively deductive reason. Because of this, it often loses itself in the construction *ad infinitum* of syllogisms in which it is often difficult to distinguish between the paralogical and the logical. But what earlier empirical practice had already discovered (without necessarily being able to articulate), and what modern thought comes to formulate, is that scientific knowledge proceeds as much from induction as deduction. Medieval scholasticism, because of its contempt for practical application, remains superbly ignorant of scientific induction, although by the force of circumstances certain scientific practices, notably medicine, always employed inductive reasoning. Whatever may have been the advances made by Christian and Islamic scholasticism, they never went beyond this reduction of human reason to its single deductive dimension. Contemporary Arab thought has still not escaped from it; thus the paralogisms and analogy that are so frequent in the practice of reasoning in all fields.

And yet, the triumph of metaphysics constitutes a permanent

invitation to the creation of a cosmogony, a general construct that claims to account for the formation of the celestial universe, terrestrial nature, human and animal life, and even society. It goes without saying that the elements of scientific knowledge, always relative, do not allow the attainment of "definitive perfection" as cosmogony claims to do. The elements of cosmogony are therefore artificially fixed by a sweeping appeal to the imaginary, indeed to the illogical. Moreover, when they serve to reinforce or even "complete" religious visions, cosmogonies run the great risk of producing intolerance and even anti-scientific fanaticism. In Christian Europe, even more so than in the land of Islam, people have been burned at the stake for refusing to embrace the cosmogony of the day and its supposedly definitively established truths.

Undoubtedly, the appeal of cosmogony—and of metaphysics—is common to all ages and did not wait for the medieval period to make itself felt. Moreover, it outlives medieval scholasticism. For the line between the philosophy of nature, which is modestly satisfied with the generalized expression at a given time of acquired scientific knowledge, and metaphysics, which claims to include everything in one sweeping gesture, is not always as easy to trace as it might theoretically appear to be. Thus the aspiration for the formulation of "general laws" governing all of nature and society can lead one to slip on the slope of cosmogony, without necessarily being aware of it: witness Engels' *The Dialectics of Nature* and Soviet "dia-mat" (dialectical materialism).

Metaphysics is the ideology *par excellence* of the tributary mode of production. The cosmogony that it inspires justifies the social order in a world where inequality of wealth and power has transparent origins. The acceptance and the reproduction of the system therefore require that the ideological order not be the object of any possible dispute; for this reason, the ideological order must also be made sacred. As a result, metaphysics becomes a major handicap to the maturation of scientific social reflection.

But however attractive and/or clever the construct that it generates may be, metaphysics always leaves an aftertaste of dissatisfaction. The reason for this, it seems, is that metaphysics proposes the impossible: the discovery, through the use of reason, of the final causes of the world. One quickly finds the limits of the power of reason; from then on, it is a question of faith. All religious minds, including Christians and Moslems, end by renouncing the exclusivity of reason in order to allow for divine inspirations, intuition, and feelings. Whether they are the complements of reason or substitutes for it, these means of recourse reinforce, if necessary, the dogma and/or the social practices that power claims to justify by their use.

Religious metaphysics has always been practiced in various versions. Without a doubt, particularly throughout the medieval period, there is a primitive practice of religion reduced to its ritual formalization, destined for the common people. Concurrently, the intellectual elite uses as its source of authority figurative interpretations that move away from the letter of the texts. Sometimes these interpretations lead along the downward path of the search for meanings "hidden" behind the transparency of the text. There are some examples of this in Arab–Islamic thought, but one finds the same thing in medieval Christian thought. It is a permanent tendency engendered by the metaphysical mind and its search for the absolute. This quest often entails abuses that become obstacles to the progress of knowledge, as when attempts are made to integrate more or less developed scientific fields into the metaphysical construct: astronomy thus becomes astrology, and mathematics the object of parascientific esotericism.

Charlatanism is therefore never far away. Moreover, the inevitable social struggles are transferred onto the field of metaphysics and of religion when it is associated with metaphysics. Here again, the popular revolts in Eastern and Western Christendom and in medieval Islam offer profound examples. Each is based upon an interpretation of metaphysics and the sacred texts which contradicts that of the ruling classes.

It is this metaphysical spirit that characterizes the entire medieval period: a search for the absolute which takes precedence over different preoccupations that in ancient times were infinitely less unified by this aspiration than they are in the medieval scholasticisms. The philosophy of nature of the first Greeks—that "spontaneous materialism" of science and praxis, as Marx and Engels called it—gives way to a total reconstruction of the world, one that is fatally imaginary, as can be foreseen.

But it seems to me that all of the elements of the metaphysical triumph exist as of the Hellenistic period. Already toward the end of the Classical Greek period, the crisis of ancient thought began. The realization of the relativity of beliefs and a need for universalism caused Socrates (469–399 B.C.) and Plato (428–347 B.C.) to remain aloof toward particular mythologies. The shortcomings of these mythologies with respect to their concepts of the individual, the soul and its possible immortality, and ethics and immanent justice, invited skepticism. They also created a malaise which Socrates believed could be overcome by recourse to human reason alone, capable in his account of discovering truth, even in the domains of the absolute. Plato was familiar with Egypt, having spent time there, and had a deep appreciation of the moral advance allowed by the Egyptian belief in the immortality of the soul.

At the same time, a need appeared for a cosmogony with universalist pretensions (because it is deduced from reasoning alone) to take the place of the multiple mythologies. Aristotle (384–322 B.C.) attempted to satisfy the new need by his classification of the components of the universe, from the stars to the sublunary world, a universe largely borrowed from the Chaldean astrological tradition.

All the elements of later metaphysics, or nearly all of them, are combined to allow the Neoplatonic synthesis of Hellenism. Plotinus (205–270 A.D.)—an Egyptian, it must be noted—produces the completed form of this synthesis. This completed expression combines, it seems to me, four groups of propositions that define the core of medieval metaphysics.

First, Plotinus affirms the predominance of the new metaphysical preoccupation: the search for absolute truth, ultimate principles, and the *raison d'être* of life and the universe. Out of this he distills the core of philosophy: wisdom. Simultaneously he affirms that this truth may be discovered through the exclusive use of deductive reason, without any recourse to particular mythologies that, after all, do not constitute sacred texts in the proper sense of the term.

Secondly, Plotinus believes that this absolute truth necessarily implies the recognition of the existence of the individualized and immortal soul, the object and subject of moral actions, by its nature universal.

Third, he calls for the completion of the search for truth

through dialectical reason by means of the practice of asceticism. Coming from distant India by way of the Persians during the time of Alexander, this appeal to intuitive feeling could have cast doubt on the unlimited power attributed to human reason. Plotinus, however, treats it as a complement: By allowing the soul to free itself of the constraints of the body and the world, ascetic practice purifies and reinforces the lucidity of reason. This is idealist reasoning in the extreme, diametrically opposed to the "spontaneous materialism" of the sciences and productive practice, according to which the confrontation with reality and the concrete effort of action on nature provide the means for improving knowledge and refining the use of reason. Some of the Neoplatonists borrow this Hindu concept and go so far as to borrow some of its characteristic forms of expression, such as metempsychosis.

Fourth, Plotinus gives in to the penchant for a cosmogonic construct, accepting the one inherited from the Chaldean tradition. Neoplatonism even goes so far as to adopt some of this cosmogony's particular traits, such as endowing the stars of the universe with superior souls, capable of action in the sublunary world and thus in human destinies. All of the astrology that has survived until this day is contained, in its basic principle and even in its details, in this proposition of Neoplatonism.

Does this grandiose synthesis constitute a step forward or a step backward with respect to ancient thought? Undoubtedly, it is both the one and the other, depending on the viewpoint that one adopts.

Three of its most important characteristics will be pointed out here.

The first characteristic: Thought accedes fully to a universalist humanism that transcends the mythologies and the specifics of peoples. Morality, the individual, and the immortal soul constitute the foundations of this humanism. The ground is thus prepared for the success of religions with a universalist vocation: Christianity and Islam.

The second characteristic: The triumph of the metaphysical spirit, affirmed in all of its dimensions, defines the mind of scholasticism and the exclusively deductive use that it makes of human reason. Considered today, from a distance, scholasticism seems to have made a largely sterile use of the capabilities of reason. Paralogism and reasoning by analogy replace the rigor imposed by the empirical confrontation with reality peculiar to the scientific search for necessarily particular and relative aspects of knowledge. The contempt for these particular and relative aspects of knowledge, in favor of metaphysical pretension, as well as the contempt for empiricism and control over nature, inspire gigantic and virtually foundationless cosmogonic constructs. Graver still is the fact that the scholastic mind tends to make "indisputable" truths of these constructs, truths that the ruling powers try to impose by force, in contempt of the value of tolerance and the demands of scientific curiosity.

The third characteristic: The Hellenistic expression of this initial formulation of medieval scholasticism is secular, in the sense that it is the exclusive product of propositions that neither rely on sacred revelations for their support nor seek to confirm such revelations. In this sense, secular Hellenistic metaphysics is "moderate," open to contradiction and conflict of expression. Later, when this metaphysics becomes the complement of the revealed religions (Christianity and Islam), it is marked by the necessity to confront sacred texts (while allowing itself, it is true, a margin of interpretation). Scholastic metaphysics becomes hardened for this reason.

Hellenism was the ideology of the ruling classes, and the dominant ideology of the ancient East for at least three centuries, and it lived beyond its prime in Eastern Christianity during the six centuries that follow, surviving in unpolished form in the West from the Roman period onward. Despite this fact, Christianity imposed itself in the region. For if the well-to-do and educated classes found satisfaction in the Neoplatonic formulation, the popular classes, who felt the same need to go beyond local mythologies, awaited their deliverance from a revelation that demonstrated, once again, its power to mobilize energies. This expectation of a messiah was reinforced by the multiple dimensions of the general societal crisis, dimensions which account for the extreme complexity of the phenomenon and of the internal conflicts that it generated.

Still, in its confrontation with Hellenism, Christianity encountered exactly the same problems that Islam would later experience.

First, it was necessary to reconcile beliefs that had become sacred, and the texts upon which these beliefs were based, with reason, fundamental to the Neoplatonic construct. In order to do so, the way had to be opened for a figurative, as opposed to literal, interpretation of the texts. Of course this opening brought about a new chapter in theological debates, and a proliferation of quarrels, which could well serve the numerous social interests (classes, peoples, powers, etc.) then in conflict.

On the other hand, Hellenistic metaphysics lent itself to a religious reinterpretation, both in a Christian and, later, Islamic context, particularly with respect to the essential matters of immortality of the soul and immanent morality. Reflection about individual responsibility and free will, always in potential conflict with divine omnipotence, and on the nature of the intervention of this power in the world, led in a short time to two solutions that came practically to define the new religious belief: unlimited individual moral responsibility, combined with the demand that the believer have a deep-seated conviction going beyond formal submission to religious rites; and a recognition that creation does not exclude the regulation of the universe by an order of laws which can be discovered by scientific reason and, consequently, the granting of exceptional status to the miracle (divine intervention outside of these laws).

The debates concerning the relationship between the universe and creation remained more open and came to naught. For if certain intellectual interpretations admitted the eternity of the world, coexisting with that of God, others, closer to popular belief, placed greater value on the literal text of Genesis. The cosmogonic constructs were the object of interminable, and to our eyes, fairly sterile debates.

Circumstances established a close relationship between the new religious form, Judaic monotheism, and the messianic expectation. These circumstances have less importance than is generally attributed to them. Nevertheless, in a short time, it was necessary to reconcile the realization of the messianic expectation with monotheistic dogma. In a situation peculiar to Christianity, the new theology was confronted with the question of the nature of Christ (divine and human), and of "divine qualities." Here again, the schools clashed incessantly with each other.

Egypt's contribution to the formation of the new Christian

world was decisive.[1] History teaches us that, in most cases, new religions are imposed by force of foreign conquest or by the will of the state and the ruling classes. The Christianization of Egypt was, however, exceptional, in that it was the exclusive product of a movement internal to Egyptian society. The richness of Christian thought in Egypt results from this confrontation with both the established powers and pagan Hellenism. Far from rejecting this erudite and subtle culture, Coptic Egypt integrates it into the new religion. The central question preoccupying the philosophers of Alexandria, whether or not they are Christian (though the non-Christian ones live in a predominately Christianized milieu), is the reconciliation of reason and faith. The agnostic Plotinus, his Christian pupil Amonius, Origen, Valentinus, Clement, and Dedemos are the great names that history has retained as the founders of gnostic philosophy. This philosophy produces an authoritative synthesis of reason and faith—the perfected form of tributary ideology—and its arguments are later taken up again by the Mutazilites.

The Egyptian synthesis proposes to classify individuals into three categories: the Gnostic elite, for whom divine inspiration comes to complete their mastery of reason; the popular masses, little preoccupied with the demands of the mind, and whose interpretation of religion remains as a result primitive and formalistic; and finally, an intermediate class capable of reconciling reason and faith, even though it rejects divine inspiration. This hierarchical division, natural for an advanced class society, had the obvious advantage of giving the thinking elite great freedom in the interpretation of dogmas; the

[1] See Mourad Kamel, *The Civilization of Coptic Egypt* (Cairo, 1961) [in Arabic].

same situation occurs in the great age of Islam, but not in the Christian West before the Renaissance. Later I shall show how Islam, when confronted with the same problems, arrived at identical answers.

The first millennium of the medieval era (from 300 B.C. to 600 A.D.) was neither poor nor sterile, despite contemporary judgments with respect to metaphysics and Hellenistic and later Eastern Christian scholasticism. Islamic metaphysics and scholasticism continue its work in the course of the first five centuries following the Hegira (from 700 to 1200 A.D.).* During this first medieval millennium, the University of Alexandria, from Ptolemy to Plotinus and until the last years of Coptic Egypt, was probably the most active center of thought in this part of the world, not only in the field of metaphysics, but also in the field of sciences, particularly astronomy and medicine, in which remarkable advances were made. The Christian expansion multiplies these intellectual centers, which included Haran in Syria, notable because its intellectual production was one of the sources for Islamic metaphysics. Of course the innumerable power struggles also fed the schools and quarrels of the six centuries of Eastern Christianity, opposing—among other things—the imperial ambitions of Byzantium to local interests (primarily Egyptian and Syrian). Once again, there is nothing dramatically different here, from that which takes place over the course of the following five Ummayid and Abbassid centuries.**

---

*The Moslem era dates from the Hegira, the forced journey of Mohammed from Mecca to Medina in 622 A.D. Dates in the Moslem calendar refer to this starting point. (Ed.)

**The Ummayid was the first dynasty of the Islamic Empire, founded in 661 A.D. It was succeeded by the Abbassid dynasty, 750–1258 A.D. (Ed.)

3. Medieval Metaphysics: The Developed Arab-Islamic Version and the Peripheral Western Version

Barely a few decades after its appearance, Islam was confronted, as a result of its conquest of the East, with a group of major
challenges to which it responded brilliantly.[2]

Islam was established on precise sacred texts, to an even more
pronounced degree than Christianity, whose Gospels, in comparison with the Koran and the Sunna (the collection of the
statements and deeds of the Prophet—the *Hadiths*), remain
fairly vague. The Moslems immediately draw up a code of laws—
the *Sharia*—that, without necessarily regulating in advance all
aspects of social life, furnish a good number of its principles and,
in certain areas, precise rules. The faith by itself is, in the
interpretation of the first Moslems of Arabia, probably crude,
just as these first adherents are themselves in their social and
cultural life. Proof of this is provided *a posteriori* by the effort
necessary to adapt the faith to the peoples of the civilized East as
they are gradually Islamized.

The Moslem state finds itself, almost from one day to the next,
the master of the Hellenized and Christian East. The challenge is
enormous at all levels: at the level of scientific and technical

[2] I will not burden the text with references to the stages of development of
Arab-Islamic thought. The works (in Arabic) of Hussein Méroué, Tayeb el-
Tizini, and Yatzji may serve here as the essential source of these references. The
debates organized in recent years around the works of Méroué and Tizini are
also present in my mind. My perspective has been elaborated in various works in
Arabic: Samir Amin, *The Crisis of Arab Society* (Cairo, 1985); *Post-Capitalism*
(Beirut, 1987); and *Concerning the Crisis of Contemporary Arab Ideology* (Al-
Fikr al-Arabi, n. 45, 1987).

knowledge (and the development of the productive forces), far beyond the level attained by the Arab nomads; at that of the complexity of social, administrative, and political relationships in the millennial state organizations of the region; at the level of Hellenistic-Christian culture, which as we have seen in the preceding pages, had elaborated an all-encompassing metaphysics and scholasticism, inspired by universalist humanism, a subtle conceptualization of belief and morality, and a reconciliation with scientific reason. But the challenge was also great at the level of the highly pronounced diversity in this region—diversity of popular realities, their linguistic and literary expressions, and the practices and beliefs that they transmit. At the same time, Persia, which had only been superficially Hellenized (quite unlike Egypt, Syria, and Mesopotamia), remained outside of Eastern Christendom—in close contact with its Christian neighbors on the one hand, but also open, to a more pronounced degree, to India. The university of Jundishapur, which also comes to play an important role in the elaboration of Islamic scholasticism, bears witness to the special status of Islamized Iran. Perhaps this difference even provides one of the keys to the mystery of this striking opposition between the Arabization of Mesopotamia, Syria, and Egypt (and later the Maghreb) and the survival of Persian to the east of the Zagros.

It was necessary to reconcile the new faith and its sacred texts with the material, political, and intellectual demands of these Hellenized-Christian and Persian worlds. This required a veritable cultural revolution, which Islam successfully brought about.

Let us note here that what the Arabs call "Greek culture" is in fact the culture of Hellenism, an already Christianized Hellenism. They remained completely ignorant of pre-Hellenistic classical Greek philosophy; they only became acquainted with Socrates, Plato, and Aristotle through Plotinus.

The Arab-Moslems immediately comprehended—we will later see by what means—that they could reconcile Hellenistic scholasticism and the new faith exactly as the Eastern Christians had done, by posing the same questions and answering them in the same way.

The story of the process of the construction of Islamic scholasticism, from the Mutazilite discourse (the *Kalam*) of the third century of the Hegira, to ibn-Rushd, the culminating point and end of this development in the sixth century of the Hegira, merits retelling.

The discourse of the Mutazilites (the *Kalam*) departs precisely from a critique of the primitive interpretation of the first Moslems, as unacceptable to the new converts as it was to the new ruling class and the Arab-Persian-Islamic intellectual elite. It is worth mentioning here at least the major questions contained in this Discourse.

It begins modestly by rejecting formalized submission to ritual as the sufficient constituent element of religious conviction. It accepts the principle of an immanent divine justice that scrutinizes the conscience, a response to a contemporary debate concerning the responsibility of the individual for sin. This leads it immediately to pose the question of free will and divine power. Supporters of free will (*al-qadaria*, the will) oppose the partisans of divine determinism (*al-jabaria, al-tassir,* divine determination) with divergent interpretations of the sacred texts. The question of free will, in turn, challenges the reigning idea of divine power. The Mutazilites opt for the Hellenistic solution: God operates by means of laws of nature (*namous al-sababia*) that he has established, and, not concerning himself with "details" (*al-jouziyat*), is loath to have recourse to "miracles." By this means they affirmed the absence of conflict between reason and revelation, since the laws of nature can be discovered through the use of reason.

Gradually the way was opened for the figurative interpretation of sacred texts. Such an interpretation was already necessary in order to reconcile the concepts of free will and of physical laws regulating the world with the concept of divine omnipotence. The problem of interpreting the meaning of the attributes of the Creator, described in anthropomorphic terms in the texts, gave rise to an opposition between partisans of the letter of sacred texts (*al-tashbih*) and the supporters of an interpretation purified of literal forms (*al-tanzih*). In the same spirit, the letter of the dogma of the resurrection of the body was rejected and replaced by the notion of a gathering of the souls (*hashr al-ajsad*). The figurative interpretation also permits a certain distance to be maintained, where necessary, with respect to the law (the *Sharia*), despite its apparently precise prescriptions. For the Koran itself, even though it is the word of God, was "created." As we would say today, it is dated and addresses the people of a certain time and place. Thus, while always being inspired by its principles, one must adapt its precepts to changing conditions. For many, this view was all but sacrilegious.

The question of creation was at the heart of these debates, which went as far as it was possible to go within the ambit of metaphysical thought. In affirming the eternity of the world, coexistent with that of the Creator, these thinkers espoused the theses of Hellenistic metaphysics, reducing the account of creation to a myth destined only to convince the mob. Many found this view still closer to sacrilege.

The *Kalam* opened the way to philosophy, conceived of as

metaphysics—that is, as the search for absolute truth. Al-Kindi, the first philosopher to write in Arabic (d. 873 A.D., 260 H.) remains prudent, recognizing the coexistence of varied paths to truth: the senses, sufficient for apprehending nature through the empirical experience; (deductive) reason, which flourishes in mathematics; and divine inspiration, the only means for gaining access to superior knowledge of the absolute. He does not posit conflict between these three paths, but, on the contrary, asserts their complementarity, on the grounds that the senses and reason have been given to humankind by God. Al-Farabi (d. 950 A.D., 339 H.), in grappling with the central question of the laws of nature (*namous al-sababia*), integrates Chaldean cosmogony into the new Islamic metaphysics. Ibn-Sina (d. 1037 A.D., 428 H.) adopts this cosmogonic perspective as well, while reinforcing it with the concept of the eternity of the universe, coexistent with that of God.

Ibn-Rushd, also known as Averroës (d. 1198 A.D., 595 H.) produced a sort of synthesis of Islamic metaphysics in the course of his polemic against the adversaries of reason, a *summa* that was later taken up almost intact by Christian scholasticism in the West. In all domains—free will, causality, the figurative interpretation of texts—ibn-Rushd placed himself in the avant-garde of Arab-Islamic thought. Did he go so far as to think that rational truth—whose independence with respect to revealed truth he proclaimed in his theory of "twofold truth"—could enter into conflict, if not with faith, at least with dogma? On these grounds, he was condemned by Moslems and, later, by the Christian heirs of his scholasticism. Did he even go so far as to cast doubt on the excesses of cosmogony? The question remains controversial. The fact that he did not treat cosmogony in his polemic may be interpreted as a rejection. But this seems unlikely to me, simply because it was accepted by everyone, including the adversaries to whom he replied (most notably Ghazzali, d. 1111 A.D., 505 H.), and because in a polemical work, it is not necessary to address theses accepted by both sides.

In another area, however, ibn-Rushd did push the limits of the possible, generating the most violent controversies by directly calling social interests into question through a challenge to the interpretation of the law (the *Sharia*). By calling for a "circumstantial" vision of the law, he opened the way for a possible separation between the state (and law) and religion. But this incipient "Protestant revolution" in Islam, if it can be spoken of it in such terms, did not have any effect. Ibn-Rushd was condemned and his books burned.

Indeed, this Islamic scholastic metaphysical construct—twin sibling of the Hellenistic and Christian constructs, the dominant ideology in the most enlightened sectors of the Arab-Persian-Islamic world during its best periods, and at times even supported by the caliph's power (as during the time of al-Mamoun, 813–833 A.D., 198–219 H.)—never had a moment of true, unchallenged triumph. The bold conclusions of the *Kalam* were quickly rejected, and ibn-Safouan reaffirmed the pre-eminence of a destiny determined in all respects by divine power, thereby opening the way for a crude, yet always popular fatalism. From al-Asari (d. 935 A.D., 324 H.) and his followers until the triumph of Ghazzali, who came to be recognized during the following eight centuries as "the proof of Islam" (*hauja al-islam*), the partisans of the letter of the texts made their position prevail and even won the ruling power over to their cause, beginning with the reign of Caliph al-Moutawakil (847 A.D., 231 H.)

The argument that was used against rational scholasticism was made to order: Reason is not sufficient and cannot lead to the sought-after absolute truth. Intuition, the heart, and divine inspiration cannot be replaced. The discovery of the limits of the power of reason could have led to a renewed questioning of metaphysics and its doomed project for arriving at absolute knowledge, but this did not happen. Renewed questioning of rational metaphysics did not lead forward (indeed, not until the European Renaissance did this forward movement begin), but rather backward, through the affirmation of a nonrational metaphysics. The result was an appeal to the techniques of asceticism, of Hindu origin, thereby inspiring the development of Sufism, the very expression of the failure of the Hellenistic-Islamic metaphysical construct.

For Sufism henceforth loudly proclaimed its skepticism with regard to reason. But it preserved the earlier preoccupation with absolute knowledge, granting it more importance than any partial knowledge, to a degree greater than at any previous time. The organization of brotherhoods (generally secret); the pursuit of practices that produce ecstatic states (*al-samar*)—rhythmic chants, sometimes drugs, and even alcohol; the adoption of the principle of blind obedience to the sheik of the group: All of this finally disturbed the ruling classes, conservative, though moderate, and jealous of centers of influence that eluded their grasp. Indeed, they would have to be naive not to suspect that this type of social reconstruction would necessarily become engaged in the multiple social and political conflicts of the time, either on its own account, or through manipulation. The punishment that the greatest Sufistic thinker, al-Halladj, suffered in 922 A.D., 309 H., bears witness to this hostility of the elites toward Sufism.*

---

*Accused of being a heretic, al-Halladj was brutally tortured and executed. (Ed.)

Islam thus unfolded over some five centuries in varied directions, which may be classified into three groupings.

The first includes a moral and rational metaphysics with universalizing aspirations, benefiting from a Hellenistic inspiration. The twin sibling of Christian scholastic metaphysics, this type of metaphysics carries out a similar reconciliation of various preoccupations: the concern with an individualized and universalist morality, the problem of confidence in deductive reason, the question of respect for sacred texts. This reconciliation also spreads into other areas, allowing the absorption of the social, economic, administrative, and political heritage of the civilized East. It is founded largely upon the use of the formal logic of language, though it does not avoid paralogism and analogy. This trait also permits it to be joined with a totalizing cosmogony (with its inevitable astrological slippings), on the one hand, and to have recourse to asceticism, if only in moderate doses. Within this general overall framework, this form of Islam allows a certain diversity of opinions and actions, creating an atmosphere unequalled in medieval times, an atmosphere relatively conducive to progress in both particular sciences and social life. This interpretation is largely that of the enlightened spheres of society—though it is not truly and fully welcomed by those in power.

For power must be mindful of what it is: the power of exploitative ruling classes. It prefers to govern the still uncouth masses, who are generally, though not always, content with simple interpretations, hardly preoccupied with philosophy and the reconciliation of reason and faith, and disposed to live according to literally construed texts and formalized ritual. This kind of religious practice, furthermore, is reconcilable with the maintenance of varied popular practices, ranging from the cult of the saints to astrology, clairvoyance, and even sorcery.

In various writings published in Arabic, I have tried to characterize the nature of the social and political struggles that shook the medieval Arab-Islamic world. Without going back over the details of my argument, I think it is possible to identify two types of conflict. There is the latent, permanent conflict between the people and authority, which bears all the characteristics of the class struggle characteristic of tributary societies. The people (peasants and small craftspeople) suffer the permanent oppression and exploitation typical of all tributary societies. They submit to it, for strategic reasons or for the well-being of their soul; but sometimes they revolt under the standard of a revolutionary interpretation of religion—neither rationalizing scholasticism nor straightforward submission to formal rites. Movements like the Karmations of the ninth century A.D. undertake a critique of the law (the *Sharia*) in order to put forth an interpretation that justifies their aspirations for equality and justice. The analogy with popular struggles against authority in other tributary systems, from medieval and Old Regime Europe to China, is obvious. But there are also conflicts within the tributary ruling class, among its professional groups or the various regional interests that it represents. These conflicts generally occupy center stage and generate wars and struggles over power.

The debates surrounding Islamic scholasticism hinge on these different kinds of conflicts and find their reflection in social thought, expressed either directly or through the prisms of literary, poetic, artistic, erudite, or popular forms. A few examples will illustrate this proposition.

In the tenth century, the Brothers of Purity (*Ikhouan al-Sifa*) undoubtedly express popular dissatisfaction with the authority of the caliph. They propose a reform that simultaneously guarantees happiness on earth (equality and justice, social solidarity) and access to eternity beyond (claiming that a moral exercise of authority is the condition for popular morality). A nostalgia for earlier times feeds their aspiration to restore the theocracy of the Rashidian caliphs (the first four caliphs), embellished, as always, with the status of a "golden age." The ambiguity of the call for a return to origins appears here in all its clarity. It is at one and the same time the expression of a project for the transformation of a reality deemed unbearable and a call for a return to past practices as the means for transformation. This call has as its foundation the absence of scientific social thought, without which it is impossible to understand the true nature of social reality. Indeed, it is not until modern times that human thought comes to the point of posing questions related to the organization of society in a manner that goes beyond simple moral debate.

Arab-Islamic social thought remains restricted to moral debate, just as social thought does in the other tributary societies, from precapitalist Europe to China. A good example is Farabi's project for an ideal city (*al-Madina al-Fadila*). Like his predecessor Hassan al-Basri (d. 728 A.D., 111 H.), Farabi believes that evil does not result from imperfections of the law (in this context, the *Sharia*), but from the shortcomings of those responsible for applying it. This is indeed an impoverished analysis.

The examples could be multiplied. Arab-Islamic social thought remains imprisoned by the objective conditions of tributary society. It goes around in circles, sometimes colliding against the wall of rationalizing scholasticism, and sometimes running into the wall of formalist submission; sometimes it gets caught in the impasse of ascetic flight. All of these detours may coexist in the works of the same individual, as in the case of the poet Abu al-Ala al-Maari (d. 1057 A.D., 449 H.), who sometimes displays confidence in reason, only to fall into fatalistic determinism or ascetic withdrawal later on.

Without a doubt, in spite of the objective limitations they face, the people of the period are as intelligent as their successors. They are therefore capable of experiencing malaise as a result of the impasse of tributary thought and of expressing, if necessary, a skepticism that prefigures a possible advance beyond it. But they do not go any farther.

Ibn-Khaldun (d. 1406 A.D., 808 H.) is unquestionably the exception; his advances in the direction of a scientific social thought are unequalled before him and unsurpassed until the eighteenth and nineteenth centuries. The impulse is there: Society is subject to nature-like laws (*namous al-sababia*), and it only remains to discover them. But the conceptual tools that ibn-Khaldun has at his disposal do not permit him to do so. The vague geographical determinations and the cycle of generations he produces, inspired by a social parapsychology, hardly lead to anything more than a vision of eternal return and of endless and unprogressive repetition. This result was perfectly acceptable to the actor-observer of the ruling classes, become skeptic, that ibn-Kaldun was; but it certainly could not nourish a truly transformative social force.

It is perhaps possible to summarize the advances made by medieval Arab-Islamic society and their limits in the few statements that follow.

First, the Arabization and Islamization of this region created the conditions for a vast society unified in language, culture, and religion, providing an objective base for the progress of the forces of production and thus for the rise of a state founded upon the tributary mode of production. The great revolution that Islam accomplished in its first age of splendor was precisely to have adapted itself to the demands of this state construct. Without this revolution, the civilized East would probably never have been Islamized and the passing of the Arabs would have been marked only by destruction, as was the case with the passing of the Mongols. Those who are nostalgic about early Islam, the period of the Prophet and the first four caliphs, refuse to understand that Islam's success came only at this price.

In the vast state, social, and cultural reconstruction of the East and the Maghreb, rational Islamic Hellenistic scholasticism filled essential functions, even though it never received true support from the ruling powers. There would be no point in enumerating all of the areas in which important progress was made: practically all of the sciences, beginning with astronomy and mathematics (the zero and decimal notation, trigonometry, and algebra are all invented), and including medicine and chemistry (which advances from alchemy to scientific chemistry). Similar advances are made in the techniques of production and in the development of the forces of production, notably through the extension of irrigation methods, as well as in the arts and letters. In all of these fields, and in the field of philosophical and social thought (within which there is an exceptional breakthrough in the direction of a social science), these brilliant moments in the rise of this new civilization take place in an environment in which diversity, controversy, open-mindedness, and even skepticism are both tolerated and welcomed.

Secondly, the primary ideological construct in this new society is a form of medieval thought, characterized—like all medieval thought—by the predominance of metaphysical preoccupations (the search for supreme knowledge), bolstered by a religious belief in need of reinforcement and even proof. Here I depart from the major contemporary Arab writers on this question (primarily Hussein Méroué and Tayeb el-Tizini). These authors base their analysis on a supposed conflict between materialism and idealism in Arab-Islamic philosophy, that they claim reflects the conflict between progressive capitalist tendencies and reactionary feudal forces. I will not repeat my comments on these propositions here. Let me simply point out that the contrast between materialism and idealism is less decisive than the popular version of Marxism suggests; and that the existence of elements of "spontaneous materialism" in the sciences, such as the doctrine of the eternity of matter, does not cancel out the fundamentally idealist character of all metaphysics.

An analysis of Arab-Islamic philosophy in terms of the conflict between feudalism and capitalism, furthermore, is simply baseless. On the contrary, the rise of this form of medieval scholasticism was an expression of the need to adapt Islam to a tributary system extending over a vast integrated space, while the resistance to it expressed the opposition of various social groups that had been victims of its rise. Among these were unquestionably those forces that represented the declining older ways of life and cultivated a nostalgia for the past, but also the popular forces, permanent victims of any prosperity founded on exploitation and oppression. Any "left"/"right" classification of their ideas must bear in mind the ambiguities of this popular resistance, which is expressed not in terms of a rational metaphysics, but through its rejection.

This hypothesis concerning the nature of Arab-Islamic thought has the advantage of providing an explanation for the seemingly curious fact that the brilliant rise of this civilization in the first centuries after the Hegira was followed by centuries of stagnation. This phenomenon is exactly the inverse of the key event in the history of the European West, the Renaissance, which opened the way for capitalist development. Arab-Islamic thought was established through a confrontation between the new ruling powers and the societies of the civilized East, the result of tributary reconstruction on a vast scale. Once the new tributary state was established and the process of Arabization and Islamization had advanced sufficiently, this confrontation could no longer contribute anything beneficial to the now-consolidated society. Arab-Islamic thought went peacefully to sleep.

This example illustrates another facet of unequal development. The progress of thought is associated with situations of confrontation and disequilibrium. Periods of stable equilibrium are periods of stagnation in thought. The flourishing of thought during the first centuries of Islam has therefore no relation to a supposed "nascent capitalism." On the contrary, it is precisely the absence of capitalist development that explains the subsequent torpor of Arab-Islamic thought.

Third, medieval Islamic scholasticism inspired to a great extent the rebirth of Christian scholasticism in the West. In the West, semi-barbaric until the eleventh century and, for this reason, incapable of assimilating Hellenistic and Eastern Christian scholasticism (which disappeared as a result of Islamization), the objective conditions that develop from the eleventh and twelfth centuries on impose a transition from the primitive stages of the tributary mode, marked by feudal fragmentation and a dispersal of power, to the advanced form represented by absolute monarchy.

During this period, the Christian West is thus ready to comprehend the full significance of Islamic scholasticism, which it adopts without the slightest uneasiness, virtually unchanged.

The debates between the Mutazilites and Asarism, and in particular the *summa* that ibn-Rushd (Averroës) composed in his polemic against Ghazzali, were read with passion and interest by Thomas Aquinas (1225–1274) and his successors as part of the revival of Christian scholasticism, which reproduces the same debates by means of the same arguments.* During the same period, Andalusian Judaism was emerging from its primitive stage and developing, under the guidance of Maimonides (d.1204 A.D., 601 H.), a metaphysical construct indistinguishable from the Islamic model. Hellenistic thought was thus discovered by the West through the mediation of the Islamic metaphysical construct. It is only later, with the exile of the Greeks of Constantinople to Rome after their city's fall in 1453, that the West begins to learn that Hellenistic thought was preceded by that of Classical Greece, whose very existence was unknown until that time.

The preceding exposition has intentionally emphasized Islamic metaphysics. This is for two reasons. First, Arab-Islamic thought is little known and poorly understood in the West, and indeed often distorted by the Eurocentric bias built into the opposition between Islam and Christianity. Secondly, and most importantly, this account has demonstrated how Islamic metaphysics completed the work of Hellenism and Eastern Christianity and perfected the tributary ideology of the region. In contrast to this model, it will be possible to judge the poverty of Western Christianity's version of metaphysics, which is only a pale, unrefined, and incomplete (peripheral) reflection of this tributary ideology.

---

*The debates between the Mutazilites and the Asharites centered around the question of free will and the determination of good and evil. Asharites adhered to the theology of al-Hasan al-Ashari (893–935 A.D.), believing that human reason was incapable of determining good and evil. (Ed.)

There are three stages in the history of Christian thought in the West: the fourth and fifth centuries, which mark the end of the Late Roman Empire in the West; the six centuries of the Dark Ages, from the sixth to the eleventh centuries; and the scholastic revival of the twelfth and thirteenth centuries.

During the first of these periods, Christian metaphysics, developed in the East, spreads in the West in simplified form. In the writings of the Egyptian Origen (in his *Contra Celsum*) a refined expression of the fundamental preoccupation of the time is found: the reconciliation of reason and revelation and of the discourse of Greek rationality and the humanist morality of the Gospels. In this text, free will and immortality of the soul are founded as much upon reason as they are upon revelation. Moreover, Origen defends the autonomy of the church from the state, calling this autonomy an essential condition for the protection of thought against the vicissitudes of power (today—if such an extrapolation is not too extreme—we would speak of the separation of civil society and the state as an essential condition for the protection of democracy). Simultaneously, Origen integrates and advocates the techniques of asceticism, later adopted by Egyptian monastics such as St. Pachomius and St. Anthony. At the same time as these fundamental debates are taking place, a number of Eastern thinkers—Athanasius, Arius, Cyril, Nestorius—develop a theology out of the controversies surrounding the nature of Christ (divine or human).

In the West, nothing comparable occurs. The contributions of St. Jerome and St. Ambrose are limited to a few epistles reminding the emperor and powerful lords of their duties, epistles whose banal content bears witness to an absence of interest in the question of the reconciliation of reason and faith. The North African St. Augustine, rightly considered the most sophisticated mind in the West, defends the letter of the texts concerning creation and refuses to admit the philosophical concept of the eternity of matter, which stands at the heart of any reconciliation of reason and faith. If St. Augustine comes to take a prominent place in the Western canon, it is probably and primarily because the Reformation found an eloquent defense for its revolt against the papacy in his plea for the separation of church and state. It is nevertheless the case that the argument on which St. Augustine bases his plea—an assertion that the designs of Providence are unknowable—comes out of the tradition of Eastern Christianity. Indeed, Western Christianity is to Eastern Christianity what Rome is to Greece.

There is nothing, or almost nothing, of note in the six centuries that follow. Kings, nobility, and an even large number of clergy are, like their subjects, illiterate. Their form of Christianity is therefore based almost exclusively on formal rites and superstition. The exception represented by the ninth-century Irishman Johannes Scotus Erigena, who treats the thesis concerning the reconciliation of reason and revelation and accepts the principle of free will, bears witness to the fact that in his island, which at his time had not yet suffered the waves of barbaric invasions, the study of the doctrines of the East had not been abandoned.

Western medieval scholasticism takes shape beginning in the twelfth century, not by chance in regions in contact with the Islamic world: Arab Andalusia and the Sicily of Frederick II. It shares certain characteristics with its Islamic source of inspiration: an unlimited reliance on syllogism and formal logic, an appreciable indifference to facts and science in general, and an appeal to reason confirm conclusions fixed in advance by revelation (principally the existence of God). But whereas the perfected metaphysics of the Islamic avant-garde purifies these conclusions of their textual dross, retaining only the abstract principle of immortality of the soul (rejecting the literal interpretation of creation, as we have seen above), Western scholasticism remains at an inferior level. Even St. Thomas Aquinas, the most advanced mind of his age, does not go as far in his *Summa contra gentiles* as ibn-Rushd (Averroës), whose conclusions he rejects as too daring and potentially threatening for the faith.

But this poverty of Western scholasticism is precisely what gave Europe its advantage. Necessarily leaving a greater sense of dissatisfaction than Islam's refined version, Western scholasticism could offer only slight resistance to the assaults of empiricism, in which Roger Bacon, restoring the importance of experience over the dialectics of scholastic syllogism, initiates a process of development independent of metaphysical discourse. Historians of the Crusades know how much the Arabs were scandalized by Frankish practices: Their "justice" founded on superstition (the ordeals) could not withstand comparison with the subtlety of the *Sharia*.* This is often forgotten today, when the *Sharia* is characterized as medieval: It was easier to get rid of a body of "law" as primitive as the Frankish one than it was to go beyond the erudite causistry of Moslem law.

Thus the triumph of Christian scholastic metaphysics in the West only lasted a short time. Hardly three centuries passed before the objective conditions were ripe for surpassing the tributary dimensions of society. With the Renaissance, beginning in the sixteenth century, the way was simultaneously prepared for capitalist development and a reexamination of the system of

---

*Without "oath-helpers" to vouch for them, those accused of crimes could only prove their innocence by surviving "ordeals" such as one-on-one combat or immersion in water with bound arms and legs. (Ed.)

medieval thought. The parallel should be noted: European feudalism, the peripheral form of the tributary mode, gave rise to a peripheral version of tributary ideology; Islamic metaphysics, heir to Hellenism and Eastern Christianity, constituted the fully developed expression of the ideology.

The paradigm that I have suggested inspires the following conclusions:

First, the break between the Age of Antiquity and the medieval era is not to be found where conventional Eurocentric history places it, that is, at the end of the Western Roman Empire in the first centuries of the Christian era. I situate this division much earlier, during the time of Alexander the Great, at the moment of the Hellenistic unification of the East (335 B.C.). The medieval era therefore includes the Hellenistic (including Roman), Byzantine, Islamic (including Ottoman), and Western Christian (feudal) worlds.

The choice of the conventional division at the end of the Roman Empire betrays a deeply rooted preconception that the Christian era marks a qualitative decisive break in world history, when in fact it does not. The break is certainly important for Europe, because it corresponds to the gradual passage from the age of Celtic, Germanic, and Slavic barbarism to organized class society, here in its feudal form. Yet it is not significant for the Byzantine and Islamic East. Its use in this context is Eurocentric and improper. The same holds true, *mutatis mutandis,* for the break represented by the Hegira. It obviously does not have the same meaning for the Islamized East—Egypt and Persia—as it does for the Arabian peninsula.

Secondly, the transition from antiquity to the medieval era does not correspond to any important transformation of the dominant mode of production, such as, for example, a passage from slavery to feudalism.

Third, the proposed division therefore belongs to the domain of the history of ideas and ideological formations. This proposition is the logical consequence of the preceding one. In a certain way, this break is thus relative. My thesis is that the elaboration of the ideology of the long tributary period begins slowly in the civilized Orient (or, to be more precise, in the civilized *Orients*) and gradually takes shape in a more coherent, more consistent, and to a certain extent definitive fashion beginning in the Hellenistic period. It thus passes through successive or coexistent forms as it crystallizes: Hellenistic, Byzantine, Islamic, and Western Christian.

Fourth, the transition from the medieval period to the modern age really corresponds to the passage to the capitalist mode. The status of religion within the system of ideas, as well as that of science, philosophy, and social ethics, becomes the object of radical reinterpretation.

II.

Tributary Culture in Other Regions of the Precapitalist World

Is the thesis outlined above concerning the central and peripheral forms of tributary culture applicable solely to the Euro-Arab-Islamic region of the world?

The Afro-Asiatic world is the non-Western, non-Christian world *par excellence*. It is also diversified, having Confucian-Taoist, Buddhist, Hindu, Islamic, and animist roots. Here, religion defined the great cultural regions in the periods preceding the modern expansion of capitalism. In comparison with this cultural plurality, the ethnic categories that nineteenth-century European anthropology and historiography tried to impose, such as the Indo-European/Semite opposition, do not carry any real weight.

If Orientalist Eurocentrism has fabricated *ex nihilo* the myth of the "Orient," this myth cannot be countered with a corresponding, inverted "Afro-Asianist" myth, but only with specific and concrete analyses of each of the sociocultural areas in the two continents. We must also avoid the two stumbling blocks of affirming immutable "traits" (of Confucianism, Islam, etc.), which easily lead to the trap of culturalism and nationalism, and of developing fragile judgments from these characteristics. To take just one example, Confucianism—formerly considered to be the cause of China's backwardness—has become in recent years the explanation for its economic take-off as well as for the Japanese and Korean "miracles."

In what follows, I will not pretend to analyze the formation of tributary ideology in each of the cultural areas enumerated. I only wish to show, on the basis of the Confucian example, the extent to which the hypothesis I have derived from Euro-Arab-Islamic history can be fruitful.

1. Confucianism, with its great systemic character, is the fully developed ideology of a fully developed tributary society, China. It is a lay philosophy, not a religion, although it has a religious undertone in that it attributes the character of a permanent human necessity to social hierarchy, following from an implicit sociopsychology that today may seem banal. The finished character of this ideology, in conjunction with the fully developed nature of the corresponding tributary mode of production, explains the great resistance it made to change (just as is the case in the West today with the ideology of economic alienation). For China to go beyond Confucianism, it has been necessary for it to go beyond the capitalist stage by means of a socialist revolution, until finally, beginning with the Cultural Revolution, this ideology could begin to lose ground.

Japan, the only non-European area of advanced capitalism, provides an exceptional field of study for a necessarily non-Eurocentric analysis of the relationships between ideology and base in social transformation.

Many contradictory remarks are made about Japan: It has lost its national character and preserved only a hollow shell or, on the contrary, it has juxtaposed or even integrated its own system of values (paternalism in enterprise, for example) with the demands of the law of profit. In fact, it can be argued that Japan advanced directly to the fully developed ideology of capitalism, with its characteristic form of market alienation, because it did not undergo the transitional phase of bourgeois individualism through which Europe passed during the Christian Reformation.

Capitalist Japan replaced an incomplete tributary society, feudal in nature. The ideology of this society was in part borrowed from China, the center of the regional civilization, though the unfinished character of the Japanese tributary system prevented it from adopting China's entire ideological construct. The relative success of Buddhism in Japan is a proof of this incomplete character of the Japanese tributary system. Buddhism, a reaction to Hinduism, is analogous to the Semitic religions in its doctrines concerning the separation of humankind and nature. But Buddhism failed in India and never managed to make a mark on Chinese ideology. Only in Japan did it succeed. However, the elements of precapitalist Japanese ideology, because they were non-European, were more difficult to integrate successfully into the new capitalist ideology. Japanese capitalist ideology recuperated above all the strictly Chinese elements of the earlier tributary ideology, as the advanced capitalist mode, the world of organization and *The One Dimensional Man,* rejoined the tributary mode, the transparency of the levy on surplus reappearing with the centralization of capital.

Michio Morishma has effectively elucidated the peripheral character of the Japanese Confucianism of the *Tokugawa Bakufu,* which parallels Japanese feudalism, itself a peripheral form of the tributary mode.[3] While Chinese Confucianism, with its

---

[3]Michio Morishima, *Capitalisme et confucianisme* (Paris: Flammarion, 1987). The *bakutu* is the feudal military system which dominated Japan throughout the dynasty of the Tokugawa Shoguns, during the five centuries preceding the Meiji restoration of the 1860s.

stress on goodness and humanism, gave rise to a civil imperial bureaucracy, the Japanese version, based upon a loyalty understood as submission to the orders of superiors, facilitated the development of a feudal military bureaucracy that became nationalistic in the modern age, just as the capitalist labor market became the modern version of a "loyalty market," in Morishima's apt phrase.

One of the remarkable elements of Confucianism is, as I have noted, its civil and nonreligious character, which makes it not unlike Hellenism. Hellenism, however, gave way to religious formulations, both Christian and Islamic, because they better satisfied popular metaphysical aspirations. In China, this religious need was expressed through peasant Taoism, a form of shamanism that provided "recipes" for acting on supernatural forces. The enlightened ruling class, on the other hand, made it a point of honor not to follow these practices: If supernatural forces exist, which is understood to be the case, the perfect Confucian must abandon the vain ambition of attempting to manipulate them. Confucianism is thus indeed a metaphysics, in the sense that it does not call into question the existence of supernatural forces; but with its sober nobility, it is a metaphysics of a type rarely equalled. While the Hellenistic and religious formulations succeed each other in time in the Euro-Arab region, they coexist in China, each having its own public: For the elites there is a nonreligious formulation, for the people a religious one. This characteristic has perhaps been an additional factor in the flexibility and hence longevity of the tributary cultural system in the region. But it has also perhaps been a factor in the relative openness of these societies to foreign contributions (Western science in Japan, Marxism in China), which were not forced to clash with rigid religious beliefs.

But if the complementary pairing of Confucianism and Taoism operated in China with the smoothness characteristic of a finished tributary civilization, in Japan the Confucian element—reduced to obedience to hierarchy—fused with Shintoism, a somewhat simplified Japanese version of Taoism, in which the deified emperor stands at the pinnacle of the hierarchy of power, symbolizing supernatural forces. The crudeness of this construct necessarily left a feeling of great dissatisfaction, which accounts for the success of Buddhist humanism among the popular masses.

The structural relationship between China and Japan—constituting a center/periphery relationship analogous to that of East and West in the Mediterranean region, as much at the level of modes of production (Japanese feudalism corresponding to that of barbarian Europe) as of ideology—has produced the same "miracle" witnessed in the Mediterranean region: the rapid maturation of capitalist development at the periphery of the system. To my mind, this parallel development constitutes definitive proof of the value of seeking universal laws that transcend local particularities. It also proves that the hypothesis of unequal development has indisputable fecundity and usefulness in this domain. If this hypothesis is accepted and employed, all Eurocentric visions of European uniqueness collapse.

Another circumstance invites us to pursue our analysis of the cultural dimension further. The entire Confucian cultural area has advanced either to capitalism, with seeming success (in Japan, South Korea, and Taiwan), or to so-called socialist revolution (China, North Korea, and Vietnam). In contrast, in the other cultural areas of Asia and Africa—the Hindu, Buddhist, Islamic, and animist worlds—despite analogous and at times even more favorable objective conditions, neither self-contained capitalist development nor revolution seems to be the order of the day in the immediate future. From this we should not conclude that the dominant ideologies in these areas, notably Islam and Hinduism, constitute absolute barriers to the crystallization of an effective and revolutionary response to the historical challenges these societies face. Islam, among other ideologies, has proven itself as flexible as its rival twin, Christianity; an Islamic "bourgeois revolution" is both necessary and possible, even though the concrete circumstances of the region's contemporary history have not allowed it so far.

Nevertheless, it is appropriate to ask whether or not Confucianism presented any relative advantages that can account for the rapid and positive evolution of the region. The civil character of Confucian ideology seems to represent one such advantage. As a result of it, Confucian societies knew only two social realities— the family on the microsocial level, the nation on the macrosocial plane—and therefore only two legitimate loyalties: familial devotion and service to the state. In a world where response to the challenge of unequal capitalist expansion requires a popular national revolution and initiative at the base, this is perhaps also an advantage. By comparison, one has only to think of the fluctuating character of Arab-Islamic revolts, oscillating between the poles of Arab nationalism and Islamic fundamentalism, or of the debilitating fragmentation caused by religious conflicts and ethnic affiliations.

2. Buddhism produces a quasi-secular metaphysics, analogous in many respects to Confucian and Hellenistic metaphysics. Hellenism, in fact, was inspired by Buddhist thought, encountered in Afghanistan. The Buddha is in effect only a sage, drawing his knowledge by his own effort from within himself; he does not claim to be an inspired prophet. Moreover, like Confucius and

the secular Hellenistic philosophers, the Buddha doubts that such a category of inspired beings can be taken seriously. He therefore concludes that humanity must elaborate its own morality without recourse to revelation, deriving its wisdom from the wisdom of human beings.

The conclusions that the Buddha reaches have the same fundamental content as those that define tributary metaphysics. The morality Buddhism proposes is universal in scope, addressing all of humanity, standing above the various religious faiths, which are not of great importance since the search for God is illusory and supernatural forces will necessarily remain unknowable. The enormous tolerance that these propositions imply is to the credit of Buddhist thought, contrasting sharply with the outbursts of fanatical fever that the so-called revealed religions frequently inspire. Furthermore, in Confucian fashion, the Buddhist morality of the "golden mean" assures respect for a conservative-reformist social order, necessary for the reproduction of tributary society.

Agnosticism in the realm of the divine does not preclude recognizing an individualized, eternal, responsible soul. In Buddhist thought, this conclusion results from the logic of sage human reflection. Born in the Hindu world, Buddhism borrowed the Hindu belief in metempsychosis. Simultaneously, the elitism characteristic of tributary ideology produced a doctrine that greatly resembles Egyptian gnosticism. Human beings are classified into two groups: "monks," capable of practicing the morality of the golden mean and of reconciling reason and metaphysical wisdom, and "commoners," content with a weakened version of social morality.

It is interesting to note that Buddhism, after having rallied vast Asiatic areas in India and China to its philosophy, ended up in

retreat in these two societies. In India, Hinduism, having presented itself as a true religion, has repressed Buddhist interpretations,
however respectful of local liturgies they may be (albeit with a
shade of elitist contempt). This retreat of Buddhism might be
compared with that of Hellenism, which was battered by Christianity. In China, the waning of Buddhism might perhaps be
explained by its too close proximity to Confucianism, which
benefited from having been produced by the national culture.

This double ebbing of Buddhism in India and China has been
accompanied by a shift in the interpretation of Buddhism, which
has come to have the status of a quasi-religion in the regions
where it has survived, from Tibet to the Indochinese peninsula.
Its fate may serve as an example of the difficulty faced by any
secular metaphysics.

PART TWO

The Culture of Capitalism

1. With the Renaissance begins the two-fold radical transformation that shapes the modern world: the crystallization of capitalist society in Europe and the European conquest of the world. These are two dimensions of the same development, and theories that separate them in order to privilege one over the other are not only insufficient and distorting but also frankly unscientific. The new world is freed from the domination of metaphysics at the same time as the material foundations for capitalist society are laid. In this way, the cultural revolution of the modern world opens the way for an explosion of scientific progress and its systematic use in the service of the development of the forces of production, and for the formation of a secularized society that can successfully carry the democratic aspiration to its conclusion. Simultaneously, Europe becomes conscious of the universal scope of its civilization, henceforth capable of conquering the world.

This new world is, for the first time in the long history of humanity, progressively unified by the fundamental rules of the capitalist economic system and founded upon the domination of private enterprise, wage labor, and free trade. It is also distinguished by the rational character of the decisions that direct not only the new enterprises but also the policies of states and of groups. These latter no longer shape their choices by the earlier exclusive logic of power but rather by economic interest, henceforth the single decisive principle. The new rationality calls for the democratic management of society and the supremacy of reason and gives rise, by force of conquest, to a unification of aspirations for a certain type of consumption and organization in social life.

In its cultural dimension, this revolution imposes itself in every domain of thought and social life, including the area of religion, whose mission is reinterpreted in conformity with the demands of the new society. Does this religious revolution not show that metaphysical belief is potentially plastic and that it is not a transhistorical cultural constant? Or rather, as some think, did only Christianity possess this flexibility?

Undoubtedly, the aspiration for rationality and universalism is not the product of the modern world. Not only has rationality always accompanied human action, but the universal concept of the human being, transcending the limits of his or her collective membership (in a race, a people, a gender, a social class) had already been produced by the great tributary ideologies, as we have seen. However, despite this, universalism had remained only a potential before the development of European capitalism, because no society had succeeded in imposing itself and its values on a worldwide scale.

For the Renaissance is not only the moment of the break with tributary ideology. It is also the point of departure for the conquest of the world by capitalist Europe. It is no coincidence that 1492 marks both the discovery of the New World and the beginnings of the Renaissance. If the period of the Renaissance marks a qualitative break in the history of humanity, it is precisely because, from that time on, Europeans become conscious of the idea that the conquest of the world by their civilization is henceforth a possible objective. They therefore develop a sense of absolute superiority, even if the actual submission of other peoples to Europe has not yet taken place. Europeans draw up the first true maps of the planet. They know of all the peoples who inhabit it, and they are the only ones to have this advantage. They know that even if a particular empire still has the military means to defend itself, they will ultimately be able to develop more powerful capabilities. From this moment on, and not before, Eurocentrism crystallizes.

We now know that the social formation that develops in Europe at this time is new, and that it is a capitalist system. We also know that this new mode of economic and social organization exhibited a conquering dynamism greatly disproportionate to that of all earlier societies. Unquestionably, the embryonic forms of capitalism (private enterprise, market exchange, free wage labor) had existed for a long time in the Mediterranean, particularly in the Arab-Islamic and Italian regions. The Mediterranean system that I discussed in the first part of this work formed, in a certain way, the prehistory of the capitalist world system. Nevertheless, this Mediterranean system did not make the qualitative leap forward to a completed capitalist form. On the contrary, the driving forces of development emigrate from the shores of the Mediterranean toward the peripheral regions of the European Atlantic northwest, thereby crossing the divide that separates the prehistory of capitalism from its later flourishing. The capitalist world system is therefore fashioned around the Atlantic, marginalizing, in turn, the old Mediterranean center.

In a certain way, then, capitalism as a potential world system did not exist until there existed a consciousness of its conquering power. In the thirteenth century, Venice was already organized along capitalist lines. But the Venetian merchants not only did not understand their society in these terms, but they also did not even suspect that their system was capable of conquering the world. During the Crusades, Christians and Moslems each believed themselves to be the keepers of the superior religious faith, but at this stage of their evolution, as evidence has proven, neither one was capable of imposing its global vision on the other. That is why the judgments of the Christians at the time of the Crusades are no more "Eurocentric" than those of the Moslems are "Islamocentric." Dante relegated Mohammed to Hell, but this was not a sign of a Eurocentric conception of the world, contrary to what Edward Said has suggested.[1] It is only a case of banal provincialism, which is something quite different, because it is symmetrical in the minds of the two opposing parties.

Maxime Rodinson has shown the difference that separates the medieval European vision of Islam—a vision woven from ignorance and fear, but not expressing any feeling of intrinsic

[1]Edward Said, *Orientalism* (New York: Pantheon, 1978). I have made numerous borrowings from his work in the course of my text: his critique of Renan on the question of Semitic languages; the evidence he presents of Orientalist claims regarding Oriental sexuality; his argument concerning the practice of making sweeping conclusions from single details; and the racist quotation from Lord Cromer.

[2]Maxime Rodinson, *Europe and the Mystique of Islam* (Seattle: University of Washington Press, 1987). See also Jean-Jacques Wardenburg, *L'Islam dans le miroir de l'Occident: Comment quelques orientalistes occidentaux se sont penchés sur l'Islam et se sont formé une image de cette religion* (The Hague: Mouton, 1963); Bernard Lewis, *The Muslim Discovery of Europe* (New York: W.W. Norton and Co., 1982); and Bernard Lewis, *Semites and Anti-Semites* (New York: W.W. Norton and Co., 1986).

European superiority, notwithstanding its view of the superiority of its own religious belief—from the Eurocentric arrogance of modern times.[2] Eurocentrism is much more than a banal manifestation of this type: It implies a theory of world history and, departing from it, a global political project.

Things begin to change with the Renaissance because a new consciousness forms in the European mind. It does not matter that at this stage, and for a long time to come, this consciousness is not the one we have today: namely, that the basis for European superiority and for its conquest of the world lies in the capitalist mode of organization of its society. At the time of their ascent the Europeans did not understand their new reality in this way. One might say that they did not know they were "building capitalism." At the time, Europeans attributed their superiority to other things: to their "Europeanness," their Christian faith, or their rediscovered Greek ancestry—which is not by chance rediscovered at this point. Eurocentrism in its entirety had already developed. In other words, the appearance of the Eurocentric dimension of modern ideology preceded the crystallization of the other dimensions that define capitalism.

The subsequent unfolding of the history of the capitalist conquest of the world showed that this conquest was not going to bring about a homogenization of the societies of the planet on the basis of the European model. On the contrary, this conquest progressively created a growing polarization at the heart of the system, crystallizing the capitalist world into fully developed centers and peripheries incapable of closing the ever widening gap, making this contradiction within "actually existing" capitalism—a contradiction insurmountable within the framework of the capitalist system—the major and most explosive contradiction of our time.

2. The new world is capitalist: It defines and recognizes itself according to the characteristics of this mode of production. But the dominant ideology that it generates cannot be organized around a lucid recognition of this nature without risking the loss of its legitimizing function. To admit the capitalist nature of the new system would be to admit that it has real, historical limits, which it will one day confront, and to underscore its internal contradictions. A dominant ideology must remove this type of destructive doubt from its field of vision. It must succeed in affirming itself as a system founded on "eternal truths" with transhistorical vocation.

The dominant ideology of the new world therefore fulfills three complementary and indissolubly linked functions. First, this ideology obscures the essential nature of the capitalist mode of production. Indeed, it replaces a lucid awareness of the economic alienation on which the reproduction of capitalist society is founded with a discourse of transhistorical, instrumental rationality.

Secondly, the ideology deforms the vision of the historical genesis of capitalism, by refusing to consider this genesis from the perspective of a search for general laws of the evolution of human society; instead, it replaces this search with a two-fold mythic construct. On the one hand, it amplifies the uniqueness of so-called European history, while on the other hand, it endows the history of other peoples with opposing "unique" traits. In this way, it succeeds in concluding that the miracle of capitalism could only have been a European one.

Thirdly, the dominant ideology refuses to link the fundamental characteristics of actually existing capitalism—that is, the center/periphery polarization, inseparable from the system itself—to capitalism's worldwide process of reproduction. Here capitalist ideology gets off cheaply by simply refusing to take the world as a unit of analysis, thus allowing it to attribute inequalities among its constituent national components to exclusively "internal" causes. In so doing, it confirms its own preconception regarding the specific, transhistorical characteristics of different peoples.

In this way, the dominant ideology legitimates at one and the same time the existence of capitalism as a social system and the worldwide inequality that accompanies it. This European ideology is constructed in stages from the Renaissance through the Enlightenment up until the nineteenth century by the invention of the eternal truths required for this legitimation. The "Christianophile" myth, the myth of Greek ancestry, and the artificial, antithetical construct of Orientalism define the new European and Eurocentric culturalism, thereby condemning it irremediably to consort with its damned soul: ineradicable racism.

Marxism is constituted as part of a contradictory movement that is at once the continuation of the philosophy of the Enlightenment and a break with this philosophy. To its credit, it successfully demystifies the fundamental economism of the dominant ideology, to such an extent that after Marx it is no longer possible to think the way people did before him. But Marxism encounters limits that it always finds difficult to surmount: It inherits a certain evolutionist perspective that prevents it from tearing down the Eurocentric veil of the bourgeois evolutionism against which it revolts. This is the case because the real historical challenge confronting actually existing capitalism remains poorly understood. In its polarizing worldwide expansion, capitalism has proposed a homogenization of the world that it cannot achieve.

The impasse is total from this point on. The contemporary

world reacts to the challenge by a desperate evasion, in a two-fold culturalist involution, Eurocentric and provincialist in the West, and "inverted Eurocentric" in the Third World. More than ever, the need for a universalism capable of meeting the challenge makes a critical examination of both of these modes of thought necessary.

I.

╼╾╼╾╼╾╼╾╼╾╼╾╼╾╼╾╼╾╼╾╼╾╼╾╼╾╼╾╼╾╼╾

The Decline of Metaphysics and the Reinterpretation of Religion

1. The Renaissance breaks with medieval thought. Modern thought distinguishes itself from that of the medieval period by renouncing the dominant metaphysical preoccupation. The importance of partial truths is systematically valorized, while the pursuit of absolute knowledge is left to amateurs. As a result, scientific research in the different domains of the knowable universe is stimulated, and because this research necessarily involves the submission of facts to empirical testing, the break between science and technology becomes relative. Simultaneously, modern science recognizes the decisive value of inductive reasoning, thereby putting an end to the errors of a reason confined strictly to deduction. It is easy now to see the relationship between this revision of intellectual priorities and the demands of the development of the forces of production in the nascent capitalist system. The earlier definition of philosophy, which, since Hellenism, had made philosophy synonymous with metaphysics, gives way to one that is inclusive and even eclectic, encompassing any reflection that is the least bit general: reflections concerning either the systems of logic that govern known phenomena or their reflections in our ways of reasoning, or the systems of aesthetic or moral value, or even the systems derived

(however improperly) from social evolutions, such as the philosophy of history.

The reason for the eclecticism of these juxtapositions cannot be found only in the opportunism of the nascent bourgeoisie, whose conciliatory spirit toward the established authorities—the absolute monarchy and the church—is well known. There is also the fact that the scholastic metaphysical construct had integrated moral preoccupation with the yearning for cosmogonic knowledge. These are two profound, permanent tendencies, immanent to the human condition and consequently ineradicable. Undoubtedly a few simplifications in the nineteenth century, the era of a triumphant bourgeoisie that no longer feared either its past masters or even the forces of the future, sought to erase moral preoccupations. American functionalism quickly moved to reduce them to banal and immediate expressions of social needs, objects of "scientific" analysis from which individuals should be "liberated" (or is it manipulated?) through "education." As for cosmogonies, which always provoke a smile, the task of maintaining that heritage has been left to the astrologers (who, of course, have never lost their job).

European Enlightenment philosophy defined the essential framework for the ideology of the European capitalist world. This philosophy is founded on a tradition of mechanistic materialism that posits chains of causal determinations. Principal among these is that science and technology determine by their autonomous progress the advance of all spheres of social life. Class struggle is removed from history and replaced by a mechanistic determination that imposes itself as an external force, a law of nature. This crude materialism, often opposed to idealism, is in fact its twin: These two ideologies are the two sides of the same coin. The claim that God (Providence) guides humanity on the road of progress or that science fulfills this function amounts to the same thing: conscious, nonalienated people, along with social classes, disappear from the scene.

For this reason, this materialism often has religious expression (witness the Freemasons or belief in the Supreme Being). It is also why the two ideologies reconcile themselves without any problem: In the United States, crass materialism determines social behavior (and its "scientific" explanation), while religious idealism survives intact in "the American soul." Bourgeois social science has never gone beyond this crass materialism, because it is necessary for the reproduction of the alienation that allows the exploitation of labor by capital. It leads necessarily to the domination of market values, which penetrate all aspects of social life and subject them to their logic. Science, technology, and organization as ideologies find their place here. At the same time, this philosophy pushes to the limit of absurdity its affirmation of a separation—in fact, opposition—between humankind and nature. It is on this level the direct opposite of Hinduism, if Hinduism is defined by the stress it places on the unity of humankind and nature. Bourgeois materialism opens the way to treating nature as a thing, even to destroying it, thereby threatening the very survival of humanity, as ecology is beginning to show us.

The autonomy of civil society is the first characteristic of the new modern world. This autonomy is founded on the separation of political authority and economic life, made opaque by the generalization of market relationships. It constitutes the qualitative difference between the new capitalist mode and all precapitalist formations. The concept of autonomous political life and thus of modern democracy and the concept of social science result from this autonomy of civil society. For the first time, society appears to be governed by laws outside of human or royal will. The evidence for this is most immediately apparent at the level of economic relationships. From now on, the attempt to discover social laws is no longer, as it was until the time of ibn-Khaldun and Montesquieu, the product of a disinterested curiosity; it is a matter of urgent necessity for the "management of capitalism." It is therefore not by chance that the new social science is constructed on the base of this all-pervasive economics.

Secularism is the direct consequence of this new autonomy of civil society, for entire areas of social life are henceforth conceivable independently of one another. The need to satisfy metaphysical yearnings is left to individual conscience, and religion loses its status as a force of formal constraint. Contrary to a widespread Eurocentric preconception, however, secularism is not peculiar to Christian society, which demanded its "liberation" from the heavy yoke of the church. Nor is it the result of the conflict between the "national" state and a church with a universal vocation. For during the Reformation, the church is in fact "nationalized" in its various forms—Anglican, Lutheran, and so forth. Nevertheless, the new fusion of church and state does not produce a new theocracy, but rather, one might say, a religious secularism. Secularism, even though it was fought by the reactionary ecclesiastical forces, did not root out belief. It even perhaps reinforced it in the long run, by freeing it of its formalist and mythological straightjackets. Christians of our time, whether or not they are intellectuals, have no problem accepting that humankind descends from apes and not from Adam and Eve.

The areas of natural science also enjoy a new autonomy, an obvious result of the weakening of metaphysical beliefs. The impulse to unify the various fields of knowledge in an all-encompassing cosmogony diminishes to the point that it becomes repugnant to scientific minds. Philosophy, once more a philosophy of nature, is content to produce a synthesis of the knowledge of the moment, a synthesis that is therefore always relative and provisional. Of course, the temptation to move from the relative to the absolute nevertheless continues to do some damage here and there. The most advanced sciences of the moment, those which are most revolutionary in their propositions, upsetting old opinions or creating pronounced material progress, tend to be imperialist, annexing more fragile areas of knowledge. Thus mechanics, the theory of Darwin, and the discovery of the atom are hastily linked to, respectively, medicine, politics, and economic life.

The new society is not, for all of that, paradise gained. Human anxiety can no more be cured by a vague positivist scientism than it could be by cosmogony or rationalizing metaphysics. Moreover, the new society remains a class society, a society marked by continual exploitation and oppression. The yearning for "another society"—for utopia, as it is called—fuses with the ever-present moral preoccupation.

2. While modern ideology frees itself from the dictatorship of metaphysics, it does not as a result suppress religious needs. The importance of metaphysical concerns (men and women being, we might say, "metaphysical animals") requires that we examine the interaction between the existence of religion, the expression of this preoccupation, and social evolution. Such an examination must depart from a perspective other than that of theology, which considers the claims of religious dogma as the immutable, defining characteristics of religion. Religions are in fact ideologically flexible and open to historical change.

Religions regulate two sets of problems: relations between

people and nature, and relationships among people. Religions therefore have a double nature, for they are at once an expression of a transhistorical human alienation and a means for legitimizing social orders shaped by historical conditions.

Different religions treat the relationship between humankind and nature in different ways, claiming either that it is a human vocation to dominate nature, or that humanity is an integral part of nature. There is a risk of making absolute judgments if too much emphasis is placed on this aspect of religion, as if this single trait constituted the essential determinant of the social evolution of religion. From this error derive the sharp, cutting judgments that have been made about Christianity, Islam, Hinduism, Buddhism, Confucianism, Taoism, and animism, claims that certain religious conceptions were "openings" to progress and others obstacles. Experience shows the vanity of these judgments, which can always be inverted.

In fact, the plasticity of religions and the possibility of adapting them in ways that allow them to justify differing relationships among people invite us to ponder the fact that ideologies formed at one moment in history can subsequently acquire vocations very different from those of their origins. To this extent, religions are transhistorical, for they can readily outlast the social conditions of their birth.

For this reason, to assert that Christianity, Islam, or Confucianism is the ideology of feudalism or the tributary mode, for example, is to make a fundamental error. These religions, in one particular interpretation, may play or have played such a role; but they may also function as ideologies of capitalism, as Christianity has in fact done through a reinterpretation of its mission.

In this domain, Eurocentrism rests upon teleology: namely,

that the entire history of Europe necessarily led to the blossoming of capitalism to the extent that Christianity, regarded as a European religion, was more favorable than other religions to the flourishing of the individual and the exercise of his or her capacity to dominate nature. The corresponding claim is that Islam, Hinduism, or Confucianism, for example, constituted obstacles to the social change necessary for capitalist development. Their plasticity is therefore denied, either because it is reserved solely for Christianity, or even because it is believed that Christianity carried the seeds of capitalist advancement within it from the beginning.

It is necessary, therefore, to reexamine, within the framework of analysis I have proposed, the revolution that Christianity has realized, one that cannot be qualified as a "bourgeois revolution." Certainly, in responding to metaphysical needs, religious faith transcends social systems. But religion is also the concrete social product of the conditions that preside over its birth. Progressive forces, which accept or even call for social change, emphasize the first of these aspects (whenever they also seek to save beliefs) and relativize the second through the free interpretation of sacred texts. Christianity, confronted with the birth of modern thought, underwent this revolution and separated itself from medieval scholasticism.

In fact, the formation of the ideology of capitalism went through different stages: the first was the adaptation of Christianity, notably by means of the Reformation. But this transformation only represented a first step, limited to certain regions of the European cultural area. Because capitalism developed early in England, its bourgeois revolution took on a religious, and therefore particularly alienated, form. Masters of the real world, the English bourgeoisie did not feel the need to develop a philoso-

phy. They contented themselves with empiricism, which comple-
mented their crude materialism; nothing more was needed to
ensure the development of the forces of production. English
political economy had this empiricism as its counterpart, functioning in place of a philosophy. However, Protestantism did not
play the same role on the European continent as it did in
England, because the development of capitalism was not sufficiently advanced there. The second wave of the formation of
capitalist ideology had, as a result, a more directly philosophical
and political cast. Neither Protestantism nor Catholicism functioned as the specific ideology of capitalism.

In fact, it was quite some time before the ideology specific to
capitalism detached itself from the earlier forms that had allowed
the passage to capitalism. Economic alienation is its primary
content, whose characteristic expression—supply and demand
as external forces regulating society—exemplifies its mystified
and mystifying nature. Once the ideology of capitalism reaches
this stage of development, it abandons its earlier forms or empties
them of their content.

Let me add a few comments to these observations concerning
the potential flexibility of religions, departing from the historical
experience of Christianity and its relationship with European
society.

First observation: My thesis is not Weber's, but the thesis of a
Weber "stood on his feet," to borrow Marx's famous observation
regarding Hegel. Weber considers capitalism to be the product
of Protestantism. I am suggesting quite the opposite: that society,
transformed by the nascent capitalist relationships of production, was forced to call the tributary ideological construct, the
construct of medieval scholasticism, into question. It was therefore real social change that brought about transformation in the

field of ideas, creating the conditions for the appearance of the ideas of the Renaissance and modern philosophy as it imposed a readjustment of religious belief—not the reverse. It took two or three centuries before the new dominant ideology crystallized, the period of transition from mercantilism to fully developed capitalism, extending from the sixteenth to the nineteenth century. The decisive step is the development of English political economy, at the moment when the Industrial Revolution and the French Revolution brought about the triumph of bourgeois power and the beginnings of the generalization of wage labor. The center of gravity shifts from metaphysics to economics, and economism becomes the content of the dominant ideology. Doesn't the person in the street believe, today more so than ever, that his or her fate depends on these "laws of supply and demand," which determine prices, employment, and all the rest, just as Providence did in earlier times?

Second observation: The religious revolution takes place on its own terms. It is not the reasoned expression of an adaptation to new times, and even less the work of cynical and clever prophets. Luther calls for a "return to the source." That is to say, he interprets medieval scholasticism as a "deviation" (a term that is always dear to ideological debate). He does not propose to "go beyond" this scholasticism, but to "erase" it in order "to restore the purity" (mythic) of its origins. This ambiguity in the religious revolution is not peculiar to the case in question. The nature of the metaphysical need to which religious belief responds always implies this distorted form of adaptation of religious belief to the demands of the times. At the same time, the ambiguity of the bourgeois revolution at the level of real society—a revolution that dethrones the tributary power and appeals to the people for help in doing so, but only in order to exploit them more efficiently in the new capitalist order—entails the stormy coexistence of the "bourgeois Reformation" and so-called heresies.

Third observation: Today we are perhaps witnessing the beginning of a second revolution in Christianity. The growing influence of the texts and beliefs of liberation theology seems to be an adaptation of Christianity to the socialist world of tomorrow. It is not by chance that this theology of liberation has been most successful in the Christian peripheries of the contemporary world—in Latin America, in the Philippines—and not in its advanced centers.

II.

~~~~~~

The Construction of Eurocentric Culture

1. Modern ideology was not constructed in the abstract ether of the pure capitalist mode of production. In fact, consciousness of the capitalist nature of the modern world came relatively late, as a result of the labor and socialist movements and their critique of nineteenth-century social organization, culminating in Marxism. At the moment when this consciousness emerged, modern ideology already had three centuries of history behind it, from the Renaissance through the Enlightenment. It had therefore expressed itself as a particularly European, rationalist, and secular ideology, while claiming a worldwide scope. The socialist critique, far from forcing bourgeois ideology to take a better measure of its historical scope and social content, led it, beginning in the nineteenth century, to strengthen its culturalist side. The Eurocentric dimension of the dominant ideology was placed even more in relief.

This dominant culture invented an "eternal West," unique since the moment of its origin. This arbitrary and mythic construct had as its counterpart an equally artificial conception of the Other (the "Orients" or "the Orient"), likewise constructed on mythic foundations. The product of this Eurocentric vision is the well-known version of "Western" history—a progression from

Ancient Greece to Rome to feudal Christian Europe to capitalist Europe—one of the most popular of received ideas. Elementary school books and popular opinion are as or even more important in the creation and diffusion of this construct as the most erudite theses developed to justify the "ancestry" of European culture and civilization.

This construct, like the analogous Orientalist construct: (i) removes Ancient Greece from the very milieu in which it unfolded and developed—the Orient—in order to annex Hellenism to Europe arbitrarily; (ii) retains the mark of racism, the fundamental basis on which European cultural unity was constructed; (iii) interprets Christianity, also annexed arbitrarily to Europe, as the principal factor in the maintenance of European cultural unity, conforming to an unscientific vision of religious phenomena; (iv) concurrently constructs a vision of the Near East and the more distant Orients on the same racist foundation, again employing an immutable vision of religion.

These four elements combined in different ways at different times. For Eurocentrism is not, properly speaking, a social theory, integrating various elements into a global and coherent vision of society and history. It is rather a prejudice that distorts social theories. It draws from its storehouse of components, retaining one or rejecting another according to the ideological needs of the moment. For example, for a long time the European bourgeoisie was distrustful—even contemptuous—of Christianity, and, because of this, amplified the myth of Greece. In what follows, I will examine the four constituent elements of the Eurocentric construct, showing how emphasis has been placed on different elements.

2. The myth of Greek ancestry performs an essential function

in the Eurocentric construct. It is an emotional claim, artificially constructed in order to evade the real question—why did capitalism appear in Europe before it did elsewhere?—by replacing it, amidst a panoply of false answers, with the idea that the Greek heritage predisposed Europe to rationality. In this myth, Greece was the mother of rational philosophy, while the "Orient" never succeeded in going beyond metaphysics.

The history of so-called Western thought and philosophy (which presupposes the existence of other, diametrically opposed thoughts and philosophies, which it calls Oriental) always begins with Ancient Greece. Emphasis is placed on the variety and conflicts of the philosophical schools, the development of thought free from religious constraints, humanism, and the triumph of reason—all without any reference to the "Orient," whose contribution to Hellenic thought is considered to be nonexistent. According to this view of history, these qualities of Greek thought are taken over by European thought beginning in the Renaissance and come of age in the modern philosophies. The two thousand or so years separating Greek antiquity from the European Renaissance are treated as a long and hazy period of transition in which no one is able to go beyond Ancient Greek thought. Christianity, which is established and conquers Europe during this transition, appears at first as a not very philosophical form of ethics, entangled for a long time in dogmatic quarrels hardly conducive to the development of the mind. It continues with these limitations, until, with the development of scholasticism in the later Middle Ages, it assimilates the newly rediscovered Aristotelianism and, with the Renaissance and Reformation, frees itself from its origins, liberating civil society from the monopoly of religion on thought. Arab-Islamic philosophy is treated in this account as if it had no other function than to transmit the Greek heritage to the Renaissance world. Moreover, Islam, in this dominant vision, could not have gone beyond the Hellenic heritage; even if it had attempted to do so, it would have failed badly.

This construct, whose origins go back to the Renaissance, filled an essential ideological function in the formation of the honest, upright bourgeois citizen, freed from the religious prejudice of the Middle Ages. At the Sorbonne, as at Cambridge, successive generations of the bourgeois elite were nourished on respect for Pericles, a respect that was even reproduced in elementary school texts. Today this emphasis on Greek ancestry is no longer as strong. Perhaps this is because the fully developed capitalist system has acquired such self-confidence that it can henceforth do without this kind of constructed legitimacy.

The construct in question is entirely mythic. Martin Bernal has demonstrated this by retracing the history of what he calls the "fabrication of Ancient Greece."[3] He recalls that the Ancient Greeks were quite conscious that they belonged to the cultural area of the ancient Orient. Not only did they recognize what they had learned from the Egyptians and the Phoenicians, but they also did not see themselves as the "anti-Orient" which Eurocentrism portrays them as being. On the contrary, the Greeks claimed that they had Egyptian ancestors—who were perhaps mythical, though that is beside the point. Bernal shows that the nineteenth-century "Hellenomania" was inspired by the racism of the Romantic movement, whose architects were moreover often the same people whom Said cites as the creators of

[3]Martin Bernal, *Black Athena: The Afroasiatic Roots of Classical Civilization. Vol. 1: The Fabrication of Ancient Greece 1785-1985* (New Brunswick: Rutgers University Press, 1987).

Orientalism. Bernal illustrates how the impulse to remove Ancient Greece from its Levantine context forced linguists into some dubious acrobatics. In fact, up to half of the Greek language was borrowed from the Egyptian and the Phoenician tongues. But linguistics invented a mysterious "Proto-Aryan" language to take the place of this borrowing, thereby safeguarding a myth dear to Eurocentrism, that of the "Aryan purity" of Greece.

The North-South split, running through the Mediterranean—which only replaced the East-West division at a late date, as we have seen—is therefore falsely projected backward. This error sometimes yields amusing results. Carthage is a Phoenician city: It is thus classified as "Oriental" and the rivalry between Rome and Carthage is said to prefigure the conquest of the "Maghreban Orient" by imperialist Europe—a curious contradiction in terms since *Maghreb* in Arabic means *West*. From the works of apologists for the French colonial conquest to the speeches of Mussolini to the textbooks still in use throughout Europe, this North-South cleavage is presented as permanent, self-evident, and inscribed in geography (and therefore—by implicit false deduction—in history). The annexation of Greece by Europe—first declared by the artists and thinkers of the Renaissance, then forgotten during the two subsequent centuries of Ottoman expansion, and declared anew by Byron and Hugo at the moment when the rising imperial powers began to divide their spoils—continues to this day with the decision of the contemporary European Community to make Athens the "cultural capital" of Europe. It is amusing to note that this homage comes at the very moment when, due to the effects of the Common Market, the last vestiges of Hellenic identity are in the process of being effaced by the endless waves of tourists, bearers of homogenizing American mass culture.

To point out this false annexation is not to reduce by one iota the importance of the "Greek miracle" in the philosophy of nature, its spontaneous materialism. However, it should be pointed out that this advance was the product of Greece's backwardness, which allowed it to make the transition from the communal mode to the tributary one successfully. Marx, whose intuition was often very keen, well in advance of his time, attributed our sympathy for Greek antiquity to the fact that it recalls our "childhood" (the childhood of all humanity, not just of Europe); Engels never failed to express an analogous sympathy not only toward the "barbarians" of the West, but also for the Iroquois and other native peoples of North America, reminders of our even more distant infancy. Later, many anthropologists— European but not Eurocentric—experienced the same feeling for other so-called "primitive" peoples, undoubtedly for the same reason.

3. The Renaissance is separated from Classical Greece by fifteen centuries of medieval history. How and on what basis is it possible, under these circumstances, to claim continuity in European culture? The nineteenth century invented the racist hypothesis for this purpose. By borrowing the methods of classification of animal species and of Darwinism and transposing them from Linnaeus, Cuvier, and Darwin to Gobineau and Renan, the human "races" were said to inherit innate characteristics that transcend social evolutions. These psychological predispositions were presented as more or less the major source of divergent social evolutions. Linguistics, a new science in formation at that time, found its inspiration for the classification of languages in the methods of the biological sciences and associated the supposedly unique characters of peoples with the characteristics of their languages.

The resulting opposition between Indo-European and Semitic (Hebrew and Arab) languages, pompously elevated to a "scientifically established" and indisputable dogma, constitutes one of the best examples of the lucubrations required for the construction of Eurocentrism. The examples could be multiplied: assertions concerning the innate taste for liberty and free and logical cast of mind of one group, contrasted with the predisposition to servility and the lack of rigor of another, etc; or Renan's claims about the "monstrous and backward" character of Semitic languages, opposed to the "perfection" of the European ones. From these premises, Eurocentrism directly deduced the contrast between Oriental philosophies, exclusively directed toward the "search for the absolute," and the humanist and scientific philosophies of "the West" (Ancient Greece and Modern Europe).

The conclusions of the racist thesis were also transposed into the domain of religion. For Christianity, after all, like Islam and other religions, is based on a search for the absolute. Moreover, Christianity was born among Orientals before it conquered the West. It thus becomes necessary to propose subtle, yet allegedly fundamental, differences that make it possible to speak of the essences of Christianity and Islam, beyond their historical expressions and transformations, as if these religions had permanent qualities that transcend history. It is amusing to point to the extent to which these so-called intrinsic characters of peoples are associated with various preconceived ideas that change with the fashion of the day. In the nineteenth century, the alleged inferiority of Semitic Orientals is based on their so-called "exuberant sexuality" (an association subsequently transferred to black peoples). Today, with the help of psychoanalysis, the same defects of Orientals are attributed to a particularly strong "sexual repression"! In this particular case, the old European anti-

Semitic prejudice was given the appearance of scientific serious-ness by combining Jews and Arabs in a single category.

This racist contrast between Europe and the Semitic Orient was continued with a series of analogous theses, based on the same model of reasoning, that posited similar oppositions be-tween the Europeans and other non-European peoples (blacks and Asiatics). However, the "Indo-European" foundation, lo-cated at the level of linguistics, was being undermined. Indians, for example, scorned because they are underdeveloped and conquered, speak Indo-European languages. Gradually a pro-gression was made from genetic racism (that is to say, based on biology) to a "geographic" racism (explained by acquired and transmissible traits produced by the geographic milieu). This geographic determinism, widely accepted by politicians, indi-viduals in authority, and popular opinion, has no scientific value whatsoever. Visiting Europe in the fourteenth century, a Europe that was still backward with respect to the Islamic world, the Arab traveller ibn-Batuta—not knowing that the course of history would so thoroughly prove him wrong—simply attribut-ed this lag to the inhospitable European climate! The inverse argument obviously has no greater value.

Judgments of this type, which attribute more or less perma-nent characteristics to a people or group of peoples and consider them to be pertinent elements for explaining their condition and evolution, always proceed from the same superficial method, which consists in drawing totalizing conclusions from single details. Their force depends largely on the detail chosen, which, when it is true and widely recognized, inspires a sweeping conclusion. A more serious analysis must be based on other grounds. The question must first be inverted: Is the alleged defining trait the cause or consequence of historical evolution?

Then the degree of pertinence of the phenomenon in question must be considered, for it might only be the simple form of expression of a more complex and flexible reality.

This mode of reasoning is not limited exclusively to Eurocentrism. Innumerable discourses on the character of the French, the English, or the Germans have been constructed in this same manner, outside of time and social development. "European" identity, constructed to distinguish it from the identity of "Others," leads almost necessarily to a search for these European traits among Europeans themselves. Each nation is defined by its closeness or distance from a "model type." Lord Cromer speaks for the entire British intellectual and ruling class when he proclaims—as if there were evidence to support the judgement—that the English and the Germans (in that order) are more "European" than, and hence obviously superior to, the French and other Latins, as well as the "semi-Asiatic" Russians. Hitler does little more than reverse the order of priority between the English and the Germans, retaining the rest of the discourse.

The most primitive form of the racist line is somewhat discredited these days. Genetic racism claims that biological traits, sometimes called "racial" characteristics, are the source of cultural diversity and create a hierarchy within that diversity. From the nineteenth century until the rise of Hitler, Europe was steeped in such inanities, even in its educated milieux. But a diluted form of racism persists, assigning durable transsocial effects to conditioning by geography and ecology. More diluted still is cultural racism, which holds that the individuals, whatever their origins, are malleable and therefore capable of assimilating another culture: the black child raised in France becomes French.

4. Recent developments since the Second World War have helped reinforce a sense of common European identity and reduced the emphasis that was previously placed on contrasts between European nations. Simultaneously, racism, especially of the genetic sort, has lost the scientific prestige that it previously had in cultured circles. Europe needed to find a new basis for its collective identity. Europe's predominantly Christian character offered a way out of this double crisis of European nationalism and racism. To my mind, the Christian revival of our period is, at least in part, an unconscious response to this situation.

But in order for Christianity to become the foundation of European identity, a sweeping, totalizing and historical interpretation had to be developed, stressing its alleged timeless characteristics and opposing it to other religions and philosophies, such as Islam and Hinduism. The theoretical presupposition had to be made that these characteristics were pertinent, in the sense that they could constitute the basis for an explanation of social evolutions.

This choice of Christianity as the basis of Europeanness obviously posed some thorny questions for social theory in general and the Eurocentric construct in particular. Since Christianity was not born on the banks of the Loire or the Rhine, it was necessary to assimilate its original form—which was Oriental, owing to the milieu in which it was established—to Eurocentric teleology. The Holy Family and the Egyptian and Syrian Church Fathers had to be made European. Non-Christian Ancient Greece also had to be assimilated into this lineage, by accentuating an alleged contrast between Greece and the ancient Orient and inventing commonalities between these civilized Greeks and the still barbaric Europeans. The core of genetic racism therefore remains. But above all, the uniqueness of Christianity had to be magnified and adorned with particular and exclusive virtues that, by simple teleology, account for the superiority of the West and its conquest of other peoples. The Eurocentric construct was thus founded on the same interpretation of religion used by all religious fundamentalisms.

Simultaneously, the West sees itself as Promethean *par excellence,* in contrast with other civilizations. Faced with the threat of an untamed nature, primitive humanity had two choices: Blend into nature or deny it. Hinduism, for example, chose the first attitude, which renders human impotence tolerable by reducing humankind to a part of nature. In contrast, Judaism and its later Christian and Islamic heirs proclaimed the original separation of humankind and nature; the superiority of humankind, made in the image of God; and the submission of nature, soulless and reduced to the object of human action. This thesis had the potential to develop into a systematic quest for the domestication of nature; but, at the first stage of development of the Semitic religions, it only formed an ideal and, with no real means for acting on nature, an appeal is made instead to a protecting God. Christianity also faced this decisive choice, all the more so because it developed in the heart of a advanced, complex society in crisis, leading it to develop the second dimension of religion. The same is true for Islam, especially once it has the responsibility of organizing a new empire.

The West's claim contains a grain of truth, since capitalist civilization is obviously Promethean. But Prometheus was Greek, not Christian. The Eurocentric, so-called Judeo-Christian, thesis glosses over what I have tried to highlight, that in the Hellenistic synthesis the Greek contribution is situated precisely at this level: The philosophy of nature calls for action upon nature, in contrast with metaphysics, which inspires a passive attitude of reflection. From this point of view, Christian or Islamic metaphysics is not fundamentally different from the metaphysics of Hinduism, for example. The Egyptian contribution to the Hellenistic construct (in its successive versions up to and including Islam) lies in the accent it places on the moral responsibility of individuals. Christianity is more marked, in a certain respect, by this last contribution, which it develops within universalist ethics stressing the love for human beings and God, than it is by Hellenistic Prometheanism, which is forgotten in the long feudal transition period in the Christian West and does not genuinely reappear until the Renaissance. In Islam, on the other hand, because Arab-Islamic civilization at its height is more advanced than the civilization of Western feudalism, the two contributions remain balanced.

One last remark concerning the ideological veil through which Europe sees itself: Christianity, by which Europe defines itself, is, like Hellenism and Islam, Oriental in origin. But the West has appropriated it, to the point that, in the popular imagination, the Holy Family is blond. It does not matter. This appropriation is not only perfectly legitimate, but has even shown itself to be fruitful. Corresponding to the peripheral character of the European feudal mode of production, this peripheral, appropriated version of Christianity has revealed itself to be remarkably flexible, allowing a rapid passage to the capitalist stage.

5. "Orientalism" is not the sum of the works of Western specialists and scholars who have studied non-European societies: This clarification is necessary to avoid misunderstandings and quarrels. This term refers to the ideological construction of a mythical "Orient," whose characteristics are treated as immuta-

ble traits defined in simple opposition to the characteristics of the "Occidental" world. The image of this "opposite" is an essential element of Eurocentrism. Edward Said has demonstrated the influence and dominance of this construct. The precision of his argument frees us from having to reproduce its details here.[4]

Once it became capitalist and developed the power to conquer, Europe granted itself the right to represent others—notably "the Orient"—and even to judge them. This right is not in itself objectionable, except from a provincialist standpoint. It is even necessary to go further. "The Orient" was incapable of representing itself with the same force that Europeans, armed with bourgeois thought, could. The Chinese of the Confucian Empire and the Arabs of the Abbassid Caliphate, like the Europeans of the Middle Ages, could analyze their own society only with the conceptual tools at their disposal, tools defined and limited by their own development.

But the representation that capitalist Europe constructs of others is, in turn, limited by the nature of capitalist development. This development was polarizing: It transformed Europe (along with North America and Japan) into the centers of the system and reduced other regions to the status of peripheries. European representations of others remain marked by this polarization, and in fact serve as a means of justifying it. Orientalism merits reproach for the simple reason that it produced false judgments. The first task for anyone who wishes to construct a genuine universalism is to detect these errors in order to determine their origins.

The critique of Orientalism that Edward Said has produced has the fault of not having gone far enough in certain respects,

[4]See Said, *Orientalism*.

and having gone too far in others. Not far enough to the extent that Said is content with denouncing Eurocentric prejudice without positively proposing another system of explanation for facts which must be accounted for. Too far, to the extent that he suggests that the vision of Europeans was already Eurocentric in the Middle Ages. This error by Said, which Maxime Rodinson has corrected by distinguishing earlier European visions of the Islamic Orient from those of the triumphant Eurocentrism of the nineteenth century, illustrates the danger of applying the concept of Eurocentrism too freely. It also shows that Said has not freed himself entirely from provincialism, leading Sadek Jalal el-Azm to qualify his analysis as "inverted Orientalism."[5]

Complementary to the right of Europeans to analyze others is the equal right of others to analyze the West. The universal right to analyze and critique entails dangers, to be sure, whose risk must nevertheless be assumed. Not only the danger of being mistaken, due to ignorance or conceptual shortcomings. But also the danger of not knowing how to take the exact measure of the various sensibilities engaged by any given statement and, as a consequence, the danger of becoming involved in false debates where vigorous polemics mask a mutual lack of understanding and impede the advancement of ideas.

Propositions concerning the cultural dimension of social reality lend themselves to this type of danger. There is always the risk of colliding with convictions situated on, for example, the terrain of religious beliefs. If the goal is to advance the project of universalism, this risk must be accepted. It is a right and a duty to analyze texts, whether or not they are considered sacred, and to

[5]Sadek Jalal el-Azm, *Orientalism and Inverted Orientalism* [in Arabic] (Beirut, 1981).

examine the interpretations that different societies have made of those texts. It is a right and a duty to explore analogies and differences, suggest origins and inspirations, and to point out evolutions. I am persuaded that no one's faith will be shaken as a result. By definition, faith answers needs to which science cannot respond.

Edward Said, for example, cites with disapproval a European Orientalist who compared Islam to the Christian Arian heresy.[6] The analysis of religions used by the social sciences is not the same as that employed by theology, even comparative theology. The question is whether a given comparison is plausible and well argued or erroneous. It must be considered at the level of science, which considers religion to be a social fact. In his study on Shiism and Sufism, the Egyptian and practicing Moslem Kamel Mustapha el-Chibi analyzes, without any discomfort, the interpenetrations of Islam, Christianity, and the other religions of the Orient.[7] To the extent that he denies the right to make this kind of comparison, Said falls, in my opinion, into the error of provincialism.

6. In imposing itself on a worldwide scale, capitalism, born in Europe, created a demand for universalism as much at the level of scientific analysis of society as at the level of elaboration of a human project capable of transcending its historical limits. Are the dominant ideology and culture produced by capitalism capable of responding to this challenge? To answer this question, it is obviously necessary at the outset to discover the axioms and

[6]Said, pp. 62-63.

[7]Kamel Mustapha el-Chibi, *Shiism and Sufism* [in Arabic] (Beirut and Cairo, 1982).

theorems on which this ideology is founded and to uncover their corollaries in every domain of social thought—from the conceptions of the contemporary world system that it inspires ("underdevelopment" and "strategies of development") to its visions of world history—just as it is necessary to understand fully the historical limits and contradictions of the system.

The dominant ideology and culture of the capitalist system cannot be reduced solely to Eurocentrism. Eurocentrism is only one dimension of the prevailing ideology, though one that has developed like an invasive cancer suppressing the essential force— that is to say, economism—in the hidden recesses of the corpulent body it has produced. It has replaced rational explanations of history with partial pseudo-theories, patched together and even self-contradictory at times, but which nevertheless function admirably in the construction of a myth that reassures Europeans, ridding their subconscious of any complex about their responsibilities.

But if Eurocentrism does not have, strictly speaking, the status of a theory, neither is it simply the sum of the prejudices, errors, and blunders of Westerners with respect to other peoples. If that were the case, it would only be one of the banal forms of ethnocentrism shared by all peoples at all times. Ignorance and mistrust of others, even chauvinism and xenophobia, testify to nothing more than the limits of the evolution of all societies that have existed until now.

The Eurocentric distortion that marks the dominant capitalist culture negates the universalist ambition on which that culture claims to be founded. As has been noted, Eurocentrism is a relatively modern construct. Bourgeois Enlightenment culture had asserted itself not only out of universalist aspirations, but also as a counterbalance to the universalist ambitions of Christianity.

The culture of the Enlightenment had no particular sympathy for the Christian Middle Ages, a period it qualified as obscurantist. Its praise for rediscovered Graeco-Roman antiquity was, at least in part, intended not so much as a means of constructing a new sense of European identity, but as a way of denouncing the obscurantism of the Christian church. But Enlightenment culture confronted a real contradiction that it could not overcome by its own means. For it was self-evident that nascent capitalism which had produced Enlightenment culture had unfolded in Europe. Moreover, this embryonic new world was in fact superior, both materially and in many other aspects, to earlier societies, both in its own territory (feudal Europe) and in other regions of the world (the neighboring Islamic Orient and the more distant Orients, which had just been discovered). The culture of the Enlightenment was unable to reconcile the fact of this superiority with its universalist ambition. On the contrary, it gradually drifted toward racism as an explanation for the contrast between it and other cultures. At the same time, it had little success in harmonizing its original European cosmopolitanism with the nationalist conflicts on which the crystallization of European capitalism came to be based. The culture of the Enlightenment thus drifted, beginning in the nineteenth century, in nationalistic directions, impoverished in comparison with its earlier cosmopolitanism.

Thus the social theory produced by capitalism gradually reached the conclusion that the history of Europe was exceptional, not in the sense that the modern world (that is to say, capitalism) was constituted there, which in itself is an undeniable fact, but because it could not have been born elsewhere. This being the case, capitalism in its Western model formed the superior prototype of social organization, a model that could be reproduced in other societies that have not had the good fortune of having initiated this superior form on the condition that these societies free themselves of the obstacles posed by their particular cultural traits, responsible for their backwardness.

The prevailing capitalist ideology thinks that this view restores the earlier universalist aspirations of Christianity, against which it had revolted in an earlier time. For Christianity, like Islam, Buddhism, and a few other religions, had been nurtured on a universalist yearning. These religions hold that the human being is by nature a creature whose vocation is identical from one individual to another. By an act of deep-seated conviction, anyone can become a human being of the highest quality, regardless of his or her origins and material and social situation. Undoubtedly, religious societies have not always functioned according to this principle of universalism: Social hypocrisy (justifying inequality) and intolerant fanaticism with regard to other religions and nonbelievers, or simply nonconformists, have been and remain the most frequent rule. But let us stay at the level of principles. The universalist aspirations of Christianity and capitalism, Europeans believed, could unite in the common expression of "Western Christian civilization."

Eurocentrism is, like all dominant social phenomena, easy to grasp in the multiplicity of its daily manifestations but difficult to define precisely. Its manifestations, like those of other prevailing social phenomena, are expressed in the most varied of areas: day-to-day relationships between individuals, political information and opinion, general views concerning society and culture, social science. These expressions are sometimes violent, leading all the way to racism, and sometimes subtle. They express themselves in the idiom of popular opinion as well as in the erudite languages of specialists on politics, the Third World, economics, history,

theology, and all the formulations of social science. I will therefore begin with this set of common ideas and opinions transmitted by the media, on which a broad consensus exists in the West,
in order to summarize the Eurocentric vision.

The European West is not only the world of material wealth
and power, including military might; it is also the site of the
triumph of the scientific spirit, rationality, and practical efficiency, just as it is the world of tolerance, diversity of opinions,
respect for human rights and democracy, concern for equality—
at least the equality of rights and opportunities—and social
justice. It is the best of the worlds that have been known up until
this time. This first thesis, which simply repeats facts which are in
themselves hardly debatable, is reinforced by the corollary thesis
that other societies—the socialist East and the underdeveloped
South—have nothing better to offer on any of the levels mentioned (wealth, democracy, or even social justice). On the contrary, these societies can only progress to the extent that they
imitate the West. And this is what they are doing, in any case,
even if they are doing it slowly and imperfectly, because of
elements of resistance based on outmoded dogmatisms (like
Marxism) or anachronistic motivations (like tribalism or religious
fundamentalism).

Consequently, it becomes impossible to contemplate any other
future for the world than its progressive Europeanization. For
the most optimistic, this Europeanization, which is simply the
diffusion of a superior model, functions as a necessary law,
imposed by the force of circumstances. The conquest of the
planet by Europe is thus justified, to the extent that it has roused
other peoples from their fatal lethargy. For others, non-European peoples have an alternative choice: either they can accept
Europeanization and internalize its demands, or, if they decide

against it, they will lead themselves to an impasse that inevitably leads to their decline. The progressive Westernization of the world is nothing more than the expression of the triumph of the humanist universalism invented by Europe.

The Westernization of the world would impose on everyone the adoption of the recipes for European superiority: free enterprise and the market, secularism and pluralist electoral democracy. It should be noted that this prescription assumes the superiority of the capitalist system, as well as this system's capacity to respond, if not to every possible challenge in the realm of the absolute, at least to all potential demands on the conceivable horizon of the future. Marxism and the socialist regimes that it has inspired are only avatars of history, brief detours in the forward march toward Westernization and capitalism.

Under these circumstances, the European West has little to learn from others. The most decisive evolutions, destined to shape the future of humanity, continue to have their origin in West, from scientific and technological progress to social advances like the recognition of the equality of men and women, from concern with ecology to the critique of the fragmented organization of labor. The tumultuous events that shake the rest of the world—socialist revolutions, anti-imperialist wars of liberation—are, despite the more radical appearance of the ambitions that nourish them, in fact less decisive for the future than the progress being made almost imperceptibly in the West. These tumultuous events are only the vicissitudes through which the peoples concerned have been compelled to pass in order to attempt to correct their backwardness.

The composite picture of Eurocentrism presented here is, by force of circumstances, simplistic, since it only retains the common denominator of varied and sometimes contradictory opinions.

The political Left and Right in the West, for example, claim to have, if not radically different conceptions of economic efficiency, social justice, and democracy, at least widely divergent views of the means necessary for progress in these areas. These differences nevertheless remain inscribed in the general framework that has been described here.

This vision of the world rests on two axioms that have not always been correctly described, both of which are erroneous in their principal formulations. The first is that internal factors peculiar to each society are decisive for their comparative evolution. The second is that the Western model of developed capitalism can be generalized to the entire planet.

No one contests the self-evident fact that worldwide capitalist expansion has been accompanied by a flagrant inequality among its partners. But are these the result of a series of accidents due for the most part to various detrimental internal factors that have slowed the process of "catching up?" Or is this inequality the product of capitalist expansion itself and impossible to surpass within the framework of this system?

The prevailing opinion is in fact that this inequality is only the result of a series of accidents, and that, consequently, the polarization between centers and peripheries can be resolved within the framework of capitalism. This opinion finds expression in the claim that "people are responsible for their condition." Is it not obvious that this simple and comfortable affirmation is analogous to the bourgeois invocation of the responsibility of individuals, designed to attribute the fate of the proletarian to his or her own deficiencies, disregarding objective social conditions?

At this point, generalizations are no longer sufficient for the development of social theory. For here two social theories and explanations of history collide which have been presented as being different, even contradictory. Nevertheless, despite this apparent divergence, we again find the Eurocentric consensus at work. For example, everyone knows that per capita income is fifteen times higher in the West than in the Third World. Bourgeois social theories and the dominant versions of Marxism interpret this fact in the same way, concluding that the productivity of labor in the West is fifteen times greater on average than at the periphery. This commonly held opinion, shared by the general public, is greatly mistaken and leads to fallacious conclusions.[8]

This consensus rests on the axiom that the achievements of different partners in the world system depend principally on "internal factors" that are favorable or unfavorable to their development within the world system, if it were possible for backward societies to "catch up " as soon as their internal factors evolved in a more propitious direction. As if integration into the world system had not rendered the internal factors unfavorable, when in fact the linkage of external factors and internal factors generally operates in a negative way, accounting for polarization of centers and peripheries. It is claimed, for example, that the West's progress was the result of class struggles, which imposed a less unequal distribution of national income and democracy. This proposition is certainly true, if somewhat out of style, given the success of right-wing ideology in asserting that inequality was the driving force of progress. But a second proposition cannot be

[8]For further discussion of the fallacious character of the discourse on underdevelopment, see my observations in *Class and Nation, Historically and in the Current Crisis* (New York and London: Monthly Review Press, 1980) pp. 131–248; *The Law of Value and Historical Materialism* (New York: Monthly Review Press, 1978), pp. 19–36, 57–82, and 107–125; and *Delinking* (London: Zed Books, forthcoming).

derived from the first: namely, that the development of similar struggles at the periphery would bring about the same result. For the international class alliances by means of which capital rules on a global scale make the development of progressive internal class alliances, particularly those of the type that allowed European society to advance, extremely difficult and improbable.

In reality, internal factors take on a decisive role in societal evolution only when a peripheralized society can free itself through delinking from the domination of international value. This implies the break-up of the transnational alliance through which the subordinated local comprador classes submit to the demands of international capital. As long as this delinking does not take place, it is futile to speak of the decisive role of internal factors, which is nothing more than a potential, and artificial to separate these factors from worldwide factors, which remain dominant.

The dominant ideology under consideration does not only propose a vision of the world. It is also a political project on a global scale: a project of homogenization through imitation and catching up.

But this project is impossible. Isn't the proof of this impossibility contained in the popular opinion that the extension of the Western way of life and consumption to the 5 billion human inhabitants of the planet would run against absolute obstacles, ecological among others? What is the point, then, in exhorting others, "Do as we do," if it is obvious from the start that it is impossible? Common sense is sufficient proof that it is impossible to imagine a world of 5 to 10 billion people benefitting from comparable high standards of living without gigantic transformations at every level and in every region of the globe, the West included. My purpose is not to characterize the necessary mode of organization of this ideal homogenized world, as socialist, for example. Let us simply acknowledge that such a world could not be managed the way it is at the present time.

Within the framework of Eurocentrism's impossible project, the ideology of the market—with its democratic complement, assumed to be almost a given—has become a veritable theology, bordering on the grotesque. For the progressive unification of the commodities and capital markets alone, without being accompanied by gigantic migrations of populations, has absolutely no chance of equalizing the economic conditions in which different peoples live. Four centuries of history of capitalist expansion have already demonstrated this fact. The last thirty years, during which the "ideology of development," founded on the fundamental hypotheses of Eurocentrism, has inspired redoubled efforts to efface what it considered to be the negative effects of colonization, have not brought about even the smallest reduction in the North-South gap.

Eurocentrism has quite simply ignored the fact that the demographic explosion of Europe, caused, like the analogous explosion in the Third World, by capitalist transformation, was accompanied by massive emigration to the Americas and a few other regions of the world. Without this massive emigration, Europe would have had to undertake its agricultural and industrial revolutions in conditions of demographic pressure analogous to those in the Third World today: The number of people of European ancestry living outside of Europe is currently twice the size of the population of the migrants' countries of origin. The litany of the market cure, invoked at every turn, comes to a dead halt here: To suggest that in a henceforth unified world, human beings, like commodities and capital, should be at home everywhere is quite simply unacceptable. The most fanatical partisans of the market suddenly find at this point an argument for the protectionism that they fustigate elsewhere as a matter of principle.

Is it necessary to moderate our indictment? Negative external factors are not always ignored. Within left-wing ideological currents in the West, it is recognized that the colonization which accompanied the European expansion favored European progress. If a few extremists only see the "civilizing role of colonization," that does not mean that this opinion is common to all of Western thought. Not everyone denies the brutality and devastating effects of the slave trade and the massacre of the American indigenous peoples. It is nevertheless the case that the dominant currents of Western social thought stress the internal transformations of European society and are content to note that identical transformations were not realized elsewhere, placing the blame almost exclusively on factors internal to these non-European societies.

The recognition of the role of colonialism in the unequal development of capitalism is not enough. For, despite this recognition, the dominant view is based on a refusal to accept the principle that the centers-peripheries contradiction constitutes the fundamental contradiction of the modern world. Certainly, until 1914 the world system was built on the basis of a centers-peripheries polarization that was accepted *de facto* at the time. Since then, this polarization is no longer accepted as such. Socialist revolutions and the successful independence struggles in former colonies are proof of this change.

To the extent that modern media places the aspiration for a better fate than that which is reserved for them in the system within the reach of all peoples, frustration mounts each day, making this contrast the most explosive contradiction of our world. Those who stubbornly refuse to call into question the

system that fosters this contrast and frustration are simply bury-
ing their heads in the sand. The world of "economists," who
administer our societies as they go about the business of "manag-
ing the world economy," is part of this artificial world. For the
problem is not one of management, but resides in the objective
necessity for a reform of the world system; failing this, the only
way out is through the worst barbarity, the genocide of entire
peoples or a worldwide conflagration. I therefore charge
Eurocentrism with an inability to see anything other than the lives
of those who are comfortably installed in the modern world.
Modern culture claims to be founded on humanist universalism.
In fact, in its Eurocentric version, it negates any such universalism. For Eurocentrism has brought with it the destruction of
peoples and civilizations who have resisted its spread. In this
sense, Nazism, far from being an aberration, always remains a
latent possibility, for it is only the extreme formulation of the
theses of Eurocentrism. If there ever were an impasse, it is that in
which Eurocentrism encloses contemporary humanity.

The dream of progress within the context of a "single world
economy" remains impossible. That is why, in the conclusion of
Class and Nation, in arguing that the centers/peripheries contradiction, immanent to actually existing capitalism, is insurmountable within the framework of this system, I suggested that the
reconstruction of an egalitarian world would require a long
transition in order to break up the world economy. Proposing an
analogy with the Roman Empire, I argued that—just as the
centralization of tribute on a wide scale throughout the Empire
became an obstacle to a process that required feudal fragmentation, the condition for the subsequent recentralization on capitalist foundations—the capitalist centralization of surplus has
today become the obstacle to the progress of peoples who are its

victims. "Delinking," understood in this context, is the only reasonable response to the challenge. Therefore, socialist experiments and the efforts of Third World countries must be analyzed and appraised in some other way than by the yardstick of Eurocentrism. The soothing discourse that declares, "They could have done as we (Westerners) did; they did not, it is their fault," eliminates from the outset the real problems encountered by the peoples who are victims of capitalist expansion.

The Eurocentric dimension of the dominant ideology constitutes a veritable paradigm of Western social science which, as Thomas Kuhn observes about all paradigms, is internalized to the point that it most often operates without anyone noticing it.[9] This is why many specialists, historians, and intellectuals can reject particular expressions of the Eurocentric construct without being embarrassed by the incoherence of the overall vision that results. Some will agree that Greece does not form the cradle of Europe; others, that Christian universalism is not different from that of other religions; still others will refuse to let themselves be locked in the Occident-Orient dichotomy. I do not contest this nor harbor any intention of making a "collective" judgment. I am only claiming that if the general laws governing the evolution of all segments of humanity are not clarified, the way is left open for the false Eurocentric ideas.

This paradigm must therefore be contrasted with another, founded on explicit hypotheses derived from general social laws, that simultaneously accounts for the precocious advance of Europe and the challenges that face the contemporary world as a result of this advance. This goal will undoubtedly seem ambitious

[9]Thomas Kuhn, *The Structure of Scientific Revolutions* (Chicago: University of Chicago Press, 1970).

to some, even if I am not attempting to propose a complete formulation of a system to replace the current one. I simply hope that the reflections proposed here will constitute a useful contribution to the elaboration of a universalism liberated from the limits of Eurocentrism.

Resistance to the critique of Eurocentrism is always extreme, for we are here entering the realm of the taboo. The calling into question of the Eurocentric dimension of the dominant ideology is more difficult to accept even than a critical challenge to its economic dimension. For the critique of Eurocentrism directly calls into question the position of the comfortable classes of this world.

This resistance is made in multiple ways. Among them is the conceptual vulgarization to which I have alluded. But there is also the recourse to an alleged realism, since, in effect, the socialist East and the underdeveloped South have not yet succeeded in proposing a better model of society and sometimes even give the impression of abandoning such an attempt in favor of rallying to the Western model. The shock provoked by this apparent adherence to the Western model has been all the greater since it has come after a long period in which Stalinism and Maoism each gave the impression that they had found the definitive answer to the question of the construction of socialism. The search for another road than the capitalist one is therefore, apparently, utopian. Allow me to suggest that the utopians are, on the contrary, those who obstinately pursue an objective—the Europeanization of the world—that is clearly impossible. Delinking is in fact the only realistic course of action. It is necessary to recognize, however, what this course entails and what hardships it imposes over the long phase of transition that it requires. It also must be understood that delinking hinges on equally necessary change in the West, as part of a total reconstruction on a global scale. In other words, patience is required, as well as a vision that extends over a much longer term than that implicitly presented by the media.

III.

Marxism and the Challenge of Actually Existing Capitalism

1. It is good form in the West today to bury Marx. Alas, those who proclaim the death of Marxism, far from surpassing its contributions to the understanding of the world, have simply shifted into reverse gear in order to return, without the slightest critical spirit, to the comfortable fold of the constructs that legitimate capitalism. We have seen the fragility of these Eurocentric constructs, as well as the frailty of the mechanistic Enlightenment materialism that underlies them. These constructs, pre-Marxist as well as post-Marxist (such as so-called neoclassical bourgeois economics), elude the essential question of the nature of the economic alienation that defines capitalism. The core of Marx's contribution is precisely this fundamental critique of the capitalist mode of production.

But the core is not the whole. The project of historical materialism is also to reinterpret world history in light of a general theory of social evolution and to open the way for transcending capitalism by means of an efficacious political strategy.

It is here that the real conflict between ideologies lies. On the one hand, we have a dominant culture that seeks to legitimize capitalism, proposes a mythical explanation of the birth of capitalism, and perpetuates itself by means of a conservative political project, accepting the world "as it is" (along with the North-South polarization that characterizes it). On the other hand, we have a still incomplete search for another culture, capable of serving as the basis for social order that can surmount the contradictions that capitalism has never overcome and can never resolve.

Marxism was founded on an awareness of the historical limits of the culture of the Enlightenment in relation to its real social content: namely, the rationalization of the national, European, and global capitalist project. It is for this reason that the tools developed by Marxism have the potential capacity to surpass the contradictions over which the Enlightenment *philosophes* stumbled. Nevertheless, "actually existing" Marxism was formed both out of and against the Enlightenment, and as a result, is marked by this origin and remains an unfinished construct.

It is necessary to go beyond the construct proposed by Marx and, to a great extent, dogmatized by the dominant currents of actual Marxism. But in order to do so without throwing the baby out with the bath water, it is essential to determine the deficiencies of classical Marxism in two key areas: its explanations of world history and the strategic vision it has of transcending capitalism.

2. Marxism did indeed advance a new explanation of the genesis of capitalism, which appealed neither to race nor to Christianity but based itself on the concepts of mode of production, base and superstructure, forces of production, and relationships of production. In contrast to bourgeois eclecticism, Marxism gives a central place to the question of universal social dynamics and at the same time proposes a total method that links

the different elements of social reality (the material base and the political and ideological superstructures). However, this double property of Marxist theory, while it gives Marxism its power, also constitutes a threat to its development. With the help of natural laziness, the temptation to find definitive answers to everything in it is great. Critique and enrichment of the theory give way to dogmatics and the analysis of texts. Limited by the knowledge available at his time, Marx developed a series of propositions that could suggest either the generality or the specificity of the succession from Graeco-Roman slavery to feudalism to capitalism. What was known in the middle of the nineteenth century about non-European peoples? Not much. And for this reason, Marx was careful about making hasty generalizations. As is well known, he declares that the slavery-feudalism-capitalism succession is peculiar to Europe. And he leaves his manuscripts dealing with the "Asiatic mode of production" in an unsystematic state, showing them to be incomplete reflections. Despite these precautions, Marxism succumbed to the temptation to extrapolate from the European example in order to fashion a universal model.

Therefore, despite Marx's precautions, Marxism yielded to the influences of the dominant culture and remained in the bosom of Eurocentrism. For a Eurocentric interpretation of Marxism, destroying its universalist scope, is not only a possibility: It exists, and is perhaps even the dominant interpretation. This Eurocentric version of Marxism is notably expressed in the famous thesis of the "Asiatic mode of production" and "the two roads": the European road, open and leading to capitalism, and the Asian road, which is blocked. It also has a related, inverted expression. In claiming the universality of the succession primitive communism–slavery–feudalism–capitalism–socialism (Stalin's theory of the five stages), the European model is applied to the entire planet, forcing everyone into an "iron corset," condemned, and rightly so, by its adversaries.

But it seems to me that it is possible to break the impasse of Eurocentrism, common to both the dominant bourgeois culture and vulgar Marxism. The thesis of unequal development, applied to the birth of capitalism, proposed to do so by suggesting that European feudalism, a peripheral form of the tributary mode, benefited from a greater flexibility which allowed the rapid success of European capitalist development. This thesis shows that at the level of the material base, constituted by the relationships of production, the feudal form was only a peripheral—primitive—form of the tributary model. In the preceding pages, I have examined this same relationship at the level of culture and ideology, finding the peripheral tributary form in Europe and the central tributary form in the Arab-Islamic Orient. The method applied equally well to other regions of the world, notably China and Japan. The productiveness of this method shows that it indeed indicates the path to follow in order to escape from the impasse of Eurocentrism.

3. The idea that Marx developed concerning the strategy for transcending capitalism is closely related to his conception of the worldwide expansion of capitalism.

Here, Marx shared the excessive optimism of his time. He believed that capitalist expansion was irresistible and that it would rapidly suppress all vestiges of earlier modes of production, as well as the social, cultural, and political forms associated with them; in a word, that this expansion would homogenize global society on the basis of a generalized social polarization (bourgeoisie/proletariat), similar from one country to the next. This belief explains his vision of a worldwide workers' revolution and his hope for proletarian internationalism. Indeed, Marx envisioned the so-called socialist transition to a classless society (communism) as a relatively brief stage, that could be perfectly mastered by the working classes.

Actually existing capitalism is nothing like this vision. The global expansion of capitalism has never made it its task to homogenize the planet. On the contrary, this expansion created a new polarization, subjecting social forms prior to capitalism at the periphery of the system to the demands of the reproduction of capital in the central formations. Reproducing and deepening this polarization stage by stage in its worldwide expansion, capitalism placed a revolution on the agenda that was not the world proletarian revolution: the revolution of the peoples who were victims of this expansion. This is a second expression of unequal development. The demand for a reexamination of capitalism, as was the case in the past for the tributary social forms, is expressed more intensely at the peripheries of the capitalist system than at its advanced centers.

In opposition to the unsatisfying eclecticism of bourgeois theory, the concept of international value could serve as the key concept of a non–Eurocentric universalist paradigm able to account for this immanent contradiction of capitalism. In effect, the concept of international value explains the double polarization that characterizes capitalism, on the one hand in the unequal distribution of income on the world scale, and on the other by the growing inequality in the distribution of income within the peripheral societies. This double aspect of national and social polarization is the real form of expression of the law of the accumulation of capital on the world scale. This polarization creates the conditions for the massive reproduction of capital at the global level, by reproducing the material conditions that allow the functioning of the transnational class alliances that bind the peripheral ruling classes to imperialism. Simultaneously, it reproduces qualitatively different social and political conditions at the centers and the peripheries. In the former case, this polarization brings about, as a result of the auto-centered character of the economy, an increase in the revenues from labor parallel to that of productivity, thereby assuring the continued functioning of the political consensus around electoral democracy. At the peripheries, this polarization separates the evolution of revenues from labor from the progress of productivity, thereby making democracy impossible. The transfer of value associated with this process of accumulation is made opaque by the price structure, which derives from the law of international value.

These conceptualizations remain widely rejected, a testimony, in my opinion, to the force of Eurocentric prejudice. For to concede the fecundity of these theses is to accept that development must take place by means of a rupture with everything that submission to the law of international value implies; in other words, it implies delinking. To accept this is to admit that development within the world capitalist system remains, for the peoples of the periphery, an impasse.

IV.

~~~~~~

The Culturalist Evasion: Provincialism and Fundamentalism

The dominant vision of history is based on one fundamental proposition: the irreducibility of historical developments—and particularly of cultures, which are said to transcend the material evolutions of different societies—to reason. The exceptional case presented by the European trajectory only confirms this general proposition.

The irreducibility of historical trajectories may be expressed either by an avowed refusal to define general laws of social evolution that are valid for humanity as a whole, or by an idealist construct—like the Eurocentric one—that opposes "Occident" and "Orient" in absolute and permanent terms. Dominant Western historiography has oscillated between these two attitudes, which have the same implications, since both effectively legitimize the status quo. Historical materialism can potentially serve as a means of escape from the impasse, provided that it is liberated from the distortions of Eurocentrism.

We are not yet at that stage. Our era is characterized by culturalist evasions as much in the West, where they take the form of praise for provincialism, as in the Third World, where they are expressed by the wave of fundamentalisms.

1. There are, in effect, two ways of approaching history. For some, emphasis should be placed on the concrete and the specific and, consequently, on the diversity of historical courses. Each history, according to this view, is unique and irreducible to any general schema. This basic option quite naturally allows a diversity of analyses, explanations, and points of view. Depending on the authors and the case under examination, a given change can be attributed to an economic, political, or ideological cause or even to an outside influence. In this vision, skepticism is the rule, and the mistrust of general constructs is great.

But there have always also been thinkers preoccupied with another order of questions, articulated around a central axis: Are there any general tendencies that govern the evolution of all societies, give a direction to their movements, and therefore make it possible to speak of world history?

The philosophy of history is the antithesis of historical science; it departs from preconceived general theses, attempting to force reality into a rigid corset, determined *a priori*. This corset can be one of various kinds: a scientistic or materialistic thesis of progress imposing itself and its demands; the antithesis of the eternal return and the cycle of civilizations; a thesis concerning the challenges a society is forced to meet or before which it succumbs; even a thesis of Providence intervening to lead its chosen people to realize its destiny.

History therefore persists as a site of fundamental and permanent debate over the means of discerning the general beyond the specific. But is this not the case with all scientific thought, which tries to go beyond the multiplicity of concrete immediate appearances in order to discover less obvious and more abstract principles?

Instead of endlessly opposing the results of limited and precise historical research and the philosophy of history, let us observe that the dominant modern historical reflections have developed in a long cycle composed of two waves, successively favorable and unfavorable to the search for the general beyond the particular.

The nineteenth century certainly gave predominance to the philosophical impulse in history. Europe's discovery of itself and its power, its conquest of the planet, the permanent revolution in the forces of production that capitalism brought about, the new freedom of thought, openly rejecting all taboos: All of this created a general atmosphere of optimism. It is not astonishing given these circumstances that nineteenth-century Europe produced all of the philosophies of history from which we still draw today, in close association with the two great movements of the time: namely, nationalism and the social movement. The former found its moral justification by invoking the "mission" of the people to which it was addressed. In this way, modern racism was introduced, in its singular ("pan-Aryan") and plural (British, French, and Germanic nationalist) forms. The social movement yielded Marxism. In varying degrees, all of these forms of thought were nourished on the scientism of the century, the almost naive expression of a religious faith in progress. This faith was assimilated into universalism, without calling into question the capitalist and European content that it transmitted. Europe was the model for everything, and the idea of calling into question its civilizing mission could only seem preposterous.

Then the pendulum returned. Fascism and world war; revolutions carried out in the name of socialism and the disappointed hopes of those who had expected the realization of the golden age; the horrors of the colonial wars, followed by the sometimes disquieting difficulties of the African and Asian powers after independence; the nuclear arms race and the specter of annihilation it has inspired: All of these developments shook the unshakeable faiths of the nineteenth century.

In their place appeared a belief in the multiplicity of ways of evolution and a call for the right to difference. Specificity seemed to triumph over supposed general laws of evolution, both as an object of analysis and as a demand. The universalist aspiration became the object of both scientific and moral distrust.

The result was an inability to produce anything more than impressionistic histories and a nurturing of simplistic philosophies of history. By default, there is nothing left but a fragmented history and a triumph of provincialism.

2. The provincialist reaction is not exclusive to Westerners. Capitalist ideology remains dominant on the world scale. This reaction therefore finds expression at the periphery of the system as well, where it appears in the inverted forms of non–European nationalist culturalisms. There, too, it is an ineffective response to the challenge at hand.

For if humanity only poses itself problems that it can solve, as Marx claims, this by no means implies that the solutions come immediately and without pain. On the contrary, the history of humankind is the story of its painful combat to transcend the contradictions arising from its own development. I therefore reject the infantile optimism of American positivism and conclude that success—that is, the capacity to find the objectively necessary solution—is not guaranteed for everyone at every moment. History is filled with the corpses of societies that did not succeed in time. The impasses resulting from the rejection of Eurocentric and imperialist universalism by means of simple negation—the affirmation of a society's own cultural "specificity"—bear witness to this danger of failure. These impasses have their own history and their concrete genesis, woven by the intersection of causes unfolding in different domains of social reality. I will give a brief illustration, departing from the critique of "Islamic fundamentalism."

How has the Arab-Islamic world, peacefully dozing since the completion of its tributary and metaphysical construct, reacted to the double challenge of Occidental material superiority—which translates into imperialism and colonization—and the new world of modern ideas?

The Arab-Islamic world is confronted today with a two-fold task: to liberate itself from imperialist domination and commit itself to a path of popular and national development (based on an authority other than that of the privileged bourgeois classes, who will only maintain its integration in the world capitalist system), thereby opening itself up to an active participation in a global socialist transformation; and, at the same time, to reconsider the system of thought it has inherited from its medieval period. We know, alas, that it has not yet truly entered the road toward its economic, social, and political liberation, in spite of the achievements of the national liberation movements and the partial victories over imperialism. But is it at least engaged in a reexamination of the system of thought associated with its historical decline?

Since the beginning of the nineteenth century, more precisely since the reign of Mohammed Ali in Egypt, there has been an awareness of this two-fold requirement for survival in the face of the challenge of the modern world. The misfortune is that until now the classes and powers responsible for the destiny of the Arab world have thought it was possible to liberate themselves from Western domination by imitating the bourgeois path of

European development, both at the level of material and social organization and at least in part, the level of ideas.

Mohammed Ali believed he could separate material modernization (undertaken by borrowing its technological elements) from calling ideology into question, which he judged to be dangerous, because it would have associated the Egyptian bourgeoisie with a power whose exclusive control he wanted to maintain. He thus opted for a "moderate conservative Islam," more formalist than preoccupied with responding to new challenges. The cultural dualism that has characterized Egypt ever since (and whose analogues can be found in many regions of the contemporary Third World) has its roots in this choice.

The *Nahda* (rebirth) was a movement that brought with it the possibility of total re-examination of the prevailing ideology.[10] It cannot be reduced to its religious dimension, roused up successively by Jamal al-Dine al-Afghani (1838–1897), Mohammed Abduh (1849–1905), and Rachid Rida (1865–1925). Its contributions to modernization in other domains of civil life are by no means small, including renovation of the language (without which Arabic would not have adapted to the new culture as it has), a critique of customs (particularly in the area of the status of women, in which the critiques of Qasim Amin, who died in 1908, have remained unequaled until the present time), a rewriting of law, and a critique of political forms (the challenge to "Oriental

[10]The history of the *Nahda* and the analysis of its works have given rise to an abundant literature. A good summary is provided by George Antonios in *Le Reveil arabe* (Paris, 1946). Among the best critical works on fundamentalism are Farag Foda, *Before the Fall* [in Arabic] (Cairo, 1983); Fouad Zakatia, *Reason and Illusion* [in Arabic] (Cairo, 1985); Hussein Ahmad Amin, *Guide du musulman malheureux* (Cairo, 1987). See also my critique of Sayyid Qutb in Samir Amin, *The Crisis of Arab Society* [in Arabic].

despotism"). Nevertheless, it is true that all of these advances, at one moment or another, collide with the question of the reform of religious interpretation.

The *Nahda's* discourse in this latter domain was both timid and ambiguous. It called for purification by means of a return to origins. So be it: Protestantism did the same. But the content that Protestantism gave to this "purification" (which did not in fact reestablish the mythic state of its origins) meshed perfectly with the future under construction. On the other hand, the discourse of the *Nadha* gave virtually no positive content to the reform it called for. Its nationalist and anti-imperialist tone, certainly justified, could not compensate for this lack, which was probably nothing more than a reflection on the level of ideas of the weaknesses of the nascent bourgeoisie. The *Nadha* had no awareness of the necessity of overturning the metaphysical cast of mind. It stayed locked in the framework of the metaphysical construct, without ever realizing that the significance of this construct had been transcended forever. Thus the very concept of secularism remained alien to the movement. The *Nadha* perhaps announced from afar a necessary religious revolution, but it did not begin it. This failure was followed necessarily by decline and even regression, from Rachid Rida to the Moslem Brotherhood and contemporary fundamentalism.

The liberal bourgeoisie, which occupied center stage in the first half of this century, remained timorous, for obvious reasons having to do with the characteristics of peripheral capitalism. It was therefore content with this cultural dualism. It did so to such a point that even bourgeois discourse could seem like national treason (for it borrows, in appearance at least, "everything" from the West, in contempt of the Islamic "heritage") or even a double game (the claim that the bourgeoisie only "pretends" to remain

Moslem). It would be unreasonable to expect anything more from the bourgeoisie. Nevertheless, while the popular forces had not yet achieved autonomy, either at the level of social and political struggle or of the elaboration of a project for society, the liberal bourgeoisie did bring about—chaotically—a few scattered fragments of modernization (in law, by modernizing the *Sharia;* in political forms; in education). There were even some bold breakthroughs, like the praise for secularism made by Ali Abderrazek, rejoicing over the occasion of the abolition of the caliphate in 1924. But these breakthroughs are shortlived.

The failure of the liberal bourgeoisie's project, at the levels of real liberation and of development, is the origin of Nasserism. As a result, Nasserism contained the potential of going further by becoming a popular national movement of renewal. But it did not do so, either in the conceptualization and carrying out of its social and political project or at the level of thought. As for its political dimension, just as Mohammed Ali had wanted to construct capitalism without relying on the bourgeoisie, Nasser gradually came to the point of wanting "socialism" without daring to entrust the people with the responsibility for its construction. Here again, the same dualism of the earlier period remains.

The failure of this most recent attempt—a material failure, above all, but one in which overt aggression of the West has a good share of responsibility—leads to the current crisis. This crisis therefore results from the failure of the "Left," meaning the ensemble of forces capable of finding a popular and national way out of the impasse. The void has been brutally filled by the "fundamentalist project"—a symptom of the crisis, not a response to it.

For fundamentalism feeds on the medieval metaphysical vision, in its most miserably impoverished version, at best that of

Ghazzali and more accurately that of the Sufis during the most lackluster moments of Arab decadence. The ideology of the movement is, from the outset, founded on a contempt for human reason; and its genuine hate for the creations of Islam in its period of grandeur—the rationalist metaphysical construct—as expressed by Sayyid Qutb (1903–1966) is more than disturbing. The fundamentalists thus give priority to an extremely formalist attachment to rituals, to the letter of sacred texts, notably the *Sharia*, and to superficial manifestations of "identity" (dress, etc.). The most banal reactionary prejudices are valorized (even if they are in conflict with more progressive interpretations from the past!), as in the case of the status of women. Ignorance is cloaked in the backward-looking myth of a golden age, preceding what is described as the "great deviation," by which is meant the construction of the Ummayid state following the Abbassid era, to which Islam and the Arab world are, however, indebted for their subsequent historical achievements. The golden age in question—left completely vague—is not linked to any coherent social project whatsoever and, as a consequence, the most flagrant contradictions are accepted in daily life (the West is rejected in its entirety, for example, but its technology is accepted without difficulty. . .). These inconsistencies and the unawareness of even the possibility of self-contradiction find their expression in repetitive writings, locked in the most insipid moralization. This is the case with the famous "Islamic political economy," which merely copies (more inaccurately than accurately) the weakest form of Western neoclassical economics. At the same time, in their organizational practices, the fundamentalists repudiate all democratic forms, even the most elementary ones, proclaiming the value of blind obedience to the "Imam" in the worst Sufistic tradition.

Numerous Arab intellectuals have brought merciless charges against this fundamentalism. They have uncovered its hidden motivations—neurotic attitudes systematically produced by peripheral capitalism, particularly among the popular strata of the petty bourgeoisie—and have unveiled its political ambiguities and ties with Saudi-American "petro-Islam." In this way, they have explained the success of Wahabism, which in other circumstances would not have passed beyond the horizon of the Central Arabian oasis.* In the same way, it has been possible to account for the support that the West had contributed to a movement that suits its purposes (support which has been hypocritically denied), owing to the incredible weakening of the Arab world it has produced through an explosion of its internal conflicts, mainly sectarian quarrels, and disputes over organizational allegiances.

The reason for the impasse is that modernity requires an abandonment of metaphysics. The failure to recognize this leads to a false construction of the question of "cultural identity" and a confused debate in which "identity" (and "heritage") are placed in absolute contrast with "modernization," viewed as synonymous with "Westernization".

This view treats the identity of peoples as immutable, disregarding the facts: The Arab-Islamic character (or better, characters) was transformed over the course of time, just like the character of "Euro-Christians" and others. Instead, an artificial, unchanging Euro-Christian identity is invented and contrasted with Arab-Islamic identity. The result is the nonsensical proposi-

---

*The Wahabi was a puritanical reform movement begun by Mohammed ibn-Abd al-Wahab (1703?–1787), which was adopted by the Saud tribe and later became the official religion of Saudi Arabia. (Ed.)

tions of Sayyid Qutb concerning secularism. According to Qutb, securalism is specifically Christian, while the alleged "uniqueness" of Islam is, on the contrary, that it knows no distinction between religion and society (*din wa dunia*). It escapes Qutb that this was also the case in medieval Europe which, for the same reasons as medieval Islam, did not separate religion from society. Ignorance permits a lot. Identity is in effect reduced to its religious dimension, and as this dimension is conceived as an immutable absolute, the simple deduction is made that the personality of peoples is itself unchanging.

I have argued that Christianity and Islam carried out a first revolution with full success. This revolution allowed both Christianity, initially a religion of popular revolt, and Islam, created on the margins of the civilized Orient, to form the central axis of a rationalist metaphysical construct conforming to the needs of an advanced tributary society. At this time, the "characters" of these religions are so similar that it is indeed difficult to qualify ibn-Rushd as Moslem, Maimonides as Jewish, and Thomas Aquinas as Christian. They are of the same intellectual period, understand one another, critique each other, and learn from one another wholeheartedly.

But Christianity carried out a second, bourgeois revolution and may perhaps be in the midst of a third. Islam is still far from making the revolution it needs. Far from calling for it, the fundamentalists are working hard to postpone it, a service for which the West is grateful.

There is certainly a way out of the impasse. But it requires more than a battle on the intellectual front alone. First, the struggle out from the real impasse at the levels of social, economic, and political practices must begin. I even believe that this transformation of the real world would bring *ipso facto* a collapse of the illusions of this impoverished metaphysics. During the rise of Nasserism, fundamentalism was unthinkable. Nevertheless, the transformation of the real world also requires giving attention to a task that, because of a shortsighted opportunism, has often been ignored: namely, the transcending of the medieval mode of thought, from which the Arab-Islamic world has yet to emerge. In this domain as in others, there can be an advantage to backwardness. Just as in the area of material activity the Third World has access to modern technologies, without having had to pass through all of the stages necessary to develop them, in the domain of thought, we are already acquainted not only with Western bourgeois thought but also with the germ of its fundamental critique, whose universal potential it is our task to develop. The real affirmation of the identity of the Arab people, like that of the other peoples of the Third World, lies on this road.

The impasse of contemporary Islamic fundamentalism is not the only one of its type. On the contrary, all signs point to analogous culturalist reactions elsewhere, from India to black Africa. In every case, it seems to me that nationalist culturalist retreat proceeds from the same method, the method of Eurocentrism: the affirmation of irreducible "unique traits" that determine the course of history, or more exactly the course of individual, incommensurable histories. These fundamentalisms are no different from Eurocentric fundamentalism, which itself tends to take the form of Christian neofundamentalism. On the contrary, they are only its reflection, its negative complement.

V.

~~~~~~~~~~~~~~~~~~~~~~~~~~~~~~~~~~~~~~

For a Truly Universal Culture

1. Substituting a new paradigm for the one on which Eurocentrism is based is a difficult, long-term task. It requires a theory of the political and a theory of culture, complementing the theory of economics, as well as a theory of their interaction. These theories are still sorely lacking, as much in bourgeois thought as in constructs of Marxist inspiration, paralyzed by a refusal to continue a task that Marx only began.

In this reconstruction, the importance of developing an analysis of culture and its function in historical development is equaled only by the difficulty of the task. Its importance derives from the fact that the dominant bourgeois mainstream in the social sciences was initially founded on an overtly culturalist philosophy of history, and then, when this philosophy gradually lost its strength of conviction, took refuge in agnosticism, refusing any search for the general beyond the specific and thus remaining under the spell of culturalism. Vulgar Marxist theories are not fundamentally different. The thesis of the so-called "two roads" tries unsuccessfully to reconcile the concepts of historical materialism with Eurocentric prejudice about the exceptional nature of European history; while the thesis of the "five stages" avoids the difficulty by minimizing specific traits to the point of artificially reducing the diversity of different historical paths to the mechanical repetition of the European schema.

But what could replace culturalist theory? The entire difficulty lies here, in the blatantly obvious inadequacies of scientific knowledge of society. I do not intend to propose a complete and coherent construct capable of answering all the questions in this domain; I have only the more modest ambition of pointing out a few of the elements that such a construct must integrate into its problematic.

2. The reconstruction of social theory along truly universalist lines must have as its base a theory of actually existing capitalism, centered on the principal contradiction generated by the world-wide expansion of this system.

This contradiction could be defined in the following way: The integration of all of the societies of our planet into the world capitalist system has created the objective conditions for universalization. However, the tendency toward homogenization, produced by the universalizing force of the ideology of commodities, that underlies capitalist development, is hindered by the very conditions of unequal accumulation. The material base of the tendency toward homogenization is the continuous extension of markets, in breadth as well as in depth. The commodity and capital markets gradually extend to the entire world and progressively take hold of all aspects of social life. The labor force, at first limited in its migrations by different social, linguistic, and legal handicaps, tends to acquire international mobility.

Cultural life being the mode of organization for the utilization of use values, the homogenization of these values by their submission to a generalized exchange value tends to homogenize culture itself. The tendency toward homogenization is the necessary consequence not of the development of the forces of production, but of the capitalist content of this development. For the progress of the forces of production in precapitalist societies did not imply the submission of use value to exchange value and hence was accompanied by a diversity of paths and methods of development. The capitalist mode implies the predominance of exchange value and hence standardization. Capitalism's tendency to homogenize functions with an almost irresistible force at the levels of industrial techniques of production, trends in consumption, lifestyle, etc., with an attenuated power in the domains of ideology and politics. It has much less influence over language usage.

What position should be taken toward this tendency toward standardization? The historically irreversible, like the Gallicization of Occitania or the adoption of Coca-Cola by the Cuban people, cannot be regretted forever. But the question arises with respect to the future. Should the tendency of capitalism toward standardization be welcomed, the way progress of the forces of production is welcomed? Should it be defended, or at least never actively opposed, keeping in mind the reactionary character of the nineteenth-century movements that sought to destroy machinery? Is the only cause for regret that this process operates through the prism of class and is, as a result, ineffective? Should we conclude that socialism will move in the same direction, only more quickly and less painfully?

There have always been two co-existing responses to this question. In the first half of his life, Marx adopted a laudatory tone when describing the progress of the forces of production, the achievements of the bourgeoisie, and the tendency toward standardization that liberates people from the limited horizons of the village. But gradually doubts crept in, and the tone of his later writings is more varied. The dominant wing of the labor movement elogized the "universal civilization" under construction. A belief in the fusion of cultures (and even of languages) predominated in the Second International: think of Esperanto. This naive cosmopolitanism, effectively disproven by World War I, reappeared after the Second World War, when Americanization came to be seen as synonymous with progress or, at the very least, modernization.

However, any fundamental critique of capitalism requires a reappraisal of this mode of consumption and life, a product of the capitalist mode of production. Such a critique is not, moreover, as utopian as is often believed: the malaise from which Western civilization suffers is ample testimony. For in fact, the tendency toward standardization implies a reinforcement of the adjustment of the superstructure to the demands of the capitalist infrastructure. This tendency diminishes the contradictions that drive the system forward and is therefore reactionary. Spontaneous resistance to this standardization thus expresses a refusal to submit to the relationships of exploitation that underlie it.

Moreover, this tendency toward standardization collides with the limits imposed by unequal accumulation. This unequal accumulation accelerates tendencies toward homogenization at the center, while it practically destroys them for the great mass of people at the periphery, who are unable to gain access to the modern mode of consumption, reserved for a small minority. For these people, who are often deprived of the elementary means of basic survival, the result is not simply malaise, but tragedy. Actually existing capitalism has therefore become a handicap to the progress of the forces of production on the world scale, for the mode of accumulation that it imposes on the periphery excludes the possibility of the periphery "catching up." This is the major reason why capitalism has been objectively transcended on the world scale.

Nevertheless, whatever opinion one may have of this model of society and its internal contradictions, it retains great force. It has a powerful attraction in the West and Japan, not only for the ruling classes, but also for the workers, testifying to the hegemony of capitalist ideology over the society as a whole. The bourgeoisies of the Third World know no other goal; they imitate the Western model of consumption, while the schools in these countries reproduce the models of organization of labor that accompany Western technologies. But the peoples of the periphery have been victims of this expanding process of the homogenization of aspirations and values. The prodigious intensification of communication by the media, now global in scope, has both quantitatively and qualitatively modified the contradiction generated by the unequal expansion of capitalism. Yearning for access to Western models of consumption has come to penetrate large numbers of the popular masses. At the same time, capitalism has revealed itself to be ever more incapable of satisfying this yearning. Societies that have liberated themselves from submission to the demands of the global expansion of capitalism must deal with this new contradiction, which is only one expression of the conflict between the socialist and capitalist tendencies.

The impasse is therefore not only ideological. It is real, the impasse of capitalism, incapable of completing the work that it has placed on the agenda of history. The crisis of social thought, in its principal dimension, is above all a crisis of bourgeois thought, which refuses to recognize that capitalism is not the "end of history," the "definitive and eternal expression of rationality." But this crisis is also an expression of the limits of Marxism which, underestimating the dimensions of the inequality immanent in the worldwide expansion of capitalism, has devised a strategy of a socialist response to these contradictions that has proven to be impossible.

In order to truly understand this contradiction, the most explosive contradiction capitalism has engendered, the centers/peripheries polarization must be placed at the heart of the analysis and not at its margin.

But after a whole series of concessions, the forces of the Left and of socialism in the West have finally given up on giving the imperialist dimension of capitalist expansion the central place that it must occupy both in critical analysis and in the development of progressive strategies. In so doing, they have been won over to bourgeois ideology in its most essential aspects: Eurocentrism and economism.

The very term imperialism has been placed under prohibition, having been judged to be "unscientific." Considerable contortions are required to replace it with a more "objective" term like "international capital" or "transnational capital." As if the world were fashioned purely by economic laws, expressions of the technical demands of the reproduction of capital. As if the state and politics, diplomacy and armies had disappeared from the scene! Imperialism is precisely an amalgamation of the requirements and laws for the reproduction of capital; the social, national, and international alliances that underlie them; and the political strategies employed by these alliances.

It is therefore indispensable to center the analysis of the contemporary world on unequal development and imperialism. Then, and only then, does it become possible to devise a strategy for a transition beyond capitalism. The obstacle is disengaging oneself from the world system as it is in reality. This obstacle is even greater for the societies of the developed center than it is for those of the periphery. And therein lies the definitive implication of imperialism. The developed central societies, because both their social composition and the advantages they enjoy from access to the natural resources of the globe are based on imperialist surpluses, have difficulty seeing the need for an overall reorganization of the world. A popular, anti-imperialist alliance capable of reversing majority opinion is as a result more difficult to construct in the developed areas of the world. In the societies of the periphery, on the other hand, disengagement from the capitalist world system is the condition for a development of the forces of production sufficient to meet the needs and demands of the majority. This fundamental difference explains why all the breaches in the capitalist system have been made from the periphery of the system. The societies of the periphery, which are entering the period of "post-capitalism" through strategies that I prefer to qualify as popular and national rather than socialist, are constrained to tackle all of the difficulties that delinking implies.

3. The principal contradiction of capitalism has thus placed an anticapitalist revolution on the agenda—a revolution that is anticapitalist because it is necessarily directed against capitalism as it is lived by those who endure its tragic consequences. But before that revolution can occur, it is necessary to finish the task that capitalism could not, and cannot, complete.

Some of these problems are not new, but rather have confronted the Russian and Chinese revolutions from the beginning. But these problems must be discussed in the light of the lessons of history, which implies something quite different from the sweeping Eurocentric judgment that socialism is bankrupt and the only alternative is a return to capitalism.[11] The same may be said,

---

[11]For my views on the national popular transition see *Delinking,* as well as "L'Etat et le développement," *Socialism in the World* 58 (1987).

mutatis mutandi, for any discussion of the lessons to be drawn from the radical movement of national liberation, which reached its apogee during the "Bandong Era" from 1955 until 1975.[12]

Without a doubt, the so-called socialist societies (which are better qualified as "popular national" societies) have not "solved" the problem, quite simply because the popular national transition will necessarily be considerably longer than anyone had imagined, since it is faced with the task of developing the forces of production in a permanent struggle with the logic of world capitalist expansion and on the basis of conflicting internal social relationships (what I have called the dialectic of three tendencies: socialist, local capitalist, and statist). In societies that have successfully made a popular national revolution (usually termed a "socialist revolution"), the dialectic of internal factors once again takes on a decisive role. Unquestionably, because the complexity of "post-capitalist" society had not been fully grasped, the Soviet experiment—such as it is—exercised a strong attraction over the peoples of the periphery for some forty years. The Maoist critique of this experiment also had considerable influence for approximately fifteen years.

Today, a better awareness of the real dimension of the challenge has already brought less naive enthusiasm and more circumspection concerning "definitive" prescriptions for development. There has been, in fact, progress in both practice and in thought, a "crisis" in the positive sense of the term and not a "failure" that would prefigure capitulation and a "return" to normalcy, that is, a reinsertion into the logic of worldwide capitalist expansion. The discouragement that has overtaken the forces of socialism in the West, who find in the situation of the

[12]See Samir Amin, *Bandoung, trente ans après* (Cairo: UNU, 1985).

"socialist" countries an alibi for their own weaknesses, has its source elsewhere, in the depths of the Western societies themselves: As long as it does not have a lucid understanding of the ravages of Eurocentrism, Western socialism will remain at a standstill.

For the peoples of the periphery, there is no other choice than that which has been the key to these so-called socialist revolutions. Certainly, things have changed greatly since 1917 or 1949. The conditions for new popular national advances in the contemporary Third World do not allow the simple reproduction of earlier approaches, sketched out in advance by a few prescriptions. In this sense, the thought and practice inspired by Marxism retain their universal vocation and their Afro-Asiatic vocation even more. In this sense, the so-called socialist countermodel, despite its current limits, retains a growing force of attraction for the countries of the periphery. The revolts against the system, from the Philippines to Korea and Brazil, passing through Iran and the Arab world, despite ambiguities and even impasses in their expression at this first stage of their development, announce other national popular advances. The skeptics, prisoners of Eurocentrism, not only had not conceived of these explosions, but had also declared their impossibility.

4. The current situation suggests an analogy with the long Hellenistic transition. In the conclusion of *Class and Nation,* we analyzed this latter transition in terms of "decadence" as opposed to "revolutionary consciousness" and suggested that the break-up of the tributary centralization of surplus and its replacement by the feudal dispersal of power, far from representing a negative "step backwards," was the condition for the subsequent rapid maturation of capitalist centralization. Today,

the liberation from the capitalist system by means of delinking constitutes in the same way the condition for the subsequent recomposition of a new universalism. On the cultural level, this three-phase dialectical movement from the false universalism of capitalist Eurocentrism to the affirmation of popular national development to the recomposition of a superior socialist universalism is accompanied by the need for delinking.

The analogy can be extended into the cultural domain. Hellenism created a universalism (regional, of course, and not global) at the level of the ruling classes of the ancient Orient. This universalism, although truncated by its class content and therefore unacceptable to the popular masses (who thus took refuge in the Christian and Moslem religions and in peasant provincialisms), foreshadowed in certain aspects the universalism developed by capitalism. This is one of the reasons that the Renaissance turned to Hellenism for inspiration. Today, isn't capitalist universalism, in spite of its Eurocentric limitations, the expression of "the" universal culture of the ruling classes? Doesn't its popular version, degraded for mass use—the more or less opulent "consumerism" of the West, and its miserable counterpart in the Third World—simultaneously generate a strong attraction and an impasse, due to the frustration it provokes? While there has been a nationalist culturalist rejection of Eurocentric universalism, at the same time, elements of a future, superior socialist universalism are crystallizing. If this crystallization progresses rapidly enough, the empty phase of negative culturalist affirmation will be shortened.

5. Because we are right in the middle of this barren phase, the stakes of the debate on Eurocentrism are considerable. Corresponding to central (European) capitalism is the completed formulation of the capitalist ideology—Eurocentric economism—

which leads to the impasse. At the peripheries, the original communal and tributary ideologies and cultures are all in a period of decline and crisis as a result of peripheralization. Without a truly universalist perspective founded on the critique of economism and enriched by the contribution of all peoples, the sterile confrontation between the Eurocentrism of some and the inverted Eurocentrisms of others will continue, in an atmosphere of destructive fanaticism.

The moral and political crisis of our time does not spare the opulent societies. Eurocentrism is in fact in crisis, despite the robust, healthy appearance of the prejudices it nurtures. Anxiety in the face of a challenge recognized as insurmountable and the risk of catastrophe it brings with it have fostered a revival of the irrational, ranging from a renewed popularity of astrology to terrorist acts. Thus, as is often the case, the reaction to a new challenge is in its first phase more negative than positive. The Eurocentric universalism of capitalism is not critiqued in order to allow the construction of a new universalism; all aspirations for universalism are rejected in favor of a "right to difference" (in this context, differences of cultures and forms of social organization) invoked as a means of evading the real problem. This is what I call "provincialism," very much in fashion today.

The view that any person has the right—and even the power—to judge others is replaced by attention to the relativity of those judgments. Without a doubt, such judgments can be erroneous, superficial, hasty, or relative. No case is ever definitively closed; debate always continues. But that is precisely the point. It is necessary to pursue debate and not to avoid it on the grounds that the views that anyone forms about others are and always will be false: that the French will never understand the Chinese (and vice versa), that men will never understand women, etc; or, in other words, that there is no human species, but only "people." Instead, the claim is made that only Europeans can truly understand Europe, Chinese China, Christians Christianity, and Moslems Islam; the Eurocentrism of one group is completed by the inverted Eurocentrism of others.

On the periphery, the recent explosion of mass political movements stirred up by culturalist nationalism, a response to the cultural aspects of modern imperialism, probably constitutes the real objective development that has provoked the sudden awareness of this cultural dimension of the problems of our time, a dimension masked by the prevailing Eurocentrism and, because of this, underestimated by classical Marxism. This explosion, however, has contributed little to the progress of critical thought. On the contrary, it has reinforced irrational emotional expressions as substitutes for analysis.

Under these circumstances, two seemingly opposed, yet actually symmetrical, literatures have been developed. At one pole are the literatures of religious fundamentalisms of every kind—Islamic, Hindu, Jewish (rarely mentioned, but it of course exists), Christian, etc.—and of provincialisms which extol the supposed superiority of folklore, all of them founded on the hypothesis of the "incommensurability" of different cultures. At the other pole is the insipid revival of bourgeois praise for capitalist society, completely inconscient of its fundamental Eurocentrism.

The cultural critique of Eurocentrism and the inverted Eurocentrisms must go beyond this dialogue of the deaf. Discussion of the cultural dimension of the problems linked to unequal development nevertheless remains difficult and muddled. The fundamental reason for this, as I have said, is the poor quality of the tools at our disposal for a scientific analysis of the relationships among the three dimensions that constitute social reality:

the economic; power and the political; and the cultural and ideological.

Is it possible to envision political evolutions here and there that are likely to favor a better dialogue and, through it, the advancement beyond capitalism toward universal socialism? The responsibility of the forces of the Left and of socialism is precisely to conceive of this and to act to make it possible.

Eurocentrism is a powerful factor in the opposite sense. Prejudice against the Third World, very much in favor today, contributes to the general shift to the right. Certain elements of the socialist movement in the West reject this shift, of course. But they do so most often in order to take refuge in another, no less Eurocentric, discourse, the discourse of traditional trade unionism, according to which only the mature (read European) working classes can be the bearers of the socialist future. An impotent discourse, in contradiction with the most obvious teachings of history.

Humanity is thus faced with a new question. If the present road of development continues, the North-South contradiction will inevitably become more and more explosive, thereby engendering, among other things, an intensified aggressive racism in the countries of developed capitalism, of which the prejudice against the Third World is only a precursor.

For the peoples of the periphery the inevitable choice is between a national popular democratic advance or a backward-looking culturalist impasse. The progressive option cannot, however, be reduced to some kind of simple prescription, for each of its three components—socialist, capitalist, and statist—is essential, partly complementing and partly conflicting with the other two. For example, the bureaucratic prescription of "state socialism" that sacrifices democracy in the name of "national development" has demonstrated that the blockages that it brings about call development itself beyond certain limits into question. But in the opposite direction, the proposal, fashionable today in the West, only to retain the democratic objective—reduced, moreover, to human rights and pluralist electoral democracy—has already manifested its ineffectiveness, in a shorter space of time than anyone imagined. As has been seen à propos of Brazil, the Philippines, and a few other experiments in progress, democracy must be linked to gigantic social transformations or perish. But these necessary transformations are of course in direct conflict with the interests of the prevailing capitalist system.

Undoubtedly, if the West, instead of standing in the way of progressive social transformations at the periphery, were to support these transformations, the element of "nationalism" contained in the project of delinking would be reduced accordingly. But this hypothesis amounts to hardly more than a pious wish. The fact is that the West has been to date the bitter adversary of any advance in this direction.

To acknowledge this as realistic and factual is to recognize that the initiative for the transformation of the world falls to the peoples of the periphery. It is they who, by disengaging themselves from world development, can force the peoples of the West to become aware of the real challenge.

But it is also to admit that the long march of popular national democracy will remain bumpy, filled with inevitable conflicts and unequal advances and setbacks. This vision of a difficult, long, and uncertain way must replace the naive image of the "construction of socialism."

The relatively negative judgment I have made concerning the West does not exclude the possibility of change here as well. By opening the debate on "other forms of development" in the West and the favorable consequences it could have for the evolution of the East and the South, I have tried to insist on the responsibilities of the Western Left as well as the possibilities that are offered to it. A lucid awareness of the destructiveness of Eurocentrism is, in this case, a prerequisite for change.

For if the right-wing version of Western ideology holds all of the responsibility for its Eurocentrism, the universalist ambition, on the other hand, has nurtured left-wing ideologies, and from the outset the bourgeois Left has forged the concepts of progress, reason, law, and justice. Moreover, the critique of Eurocentric capitalism is not without its echo at the center. No Great Wall separates the center from the periphery in the world system. Were not Mao, Che, and Fanon heroes of the progressive young people of the West at one time?

It is for this reason that I have addressed these pages to the intellectuals of the Western Left, in the hope of opening a genuine dialogue, because the role of Europe can be more decisive than is often realized.

Obedience to the logic of the world economy demands in effect that a police force assume the responsibility for repressing the revolts of the peoples of the periphery, victims of the system, and of averting the danger that the socialist states might benefit from possible alliances with these peoples, a function that cannot be filled by anyone other than the United States. The construction of a European neo-imperialism, relieving America from its guard duty, remains an impossible dream for the conceivable future. The Atlanticism that this pure capitalist logic thus implies inevitably reduces the European role to staying within the strict limits of a mercantile competition between Europe, Japan, and the United States, without aspiring for any kind of cultural, ideological, political, and military autonomy. But in these circumstances, Europe remains threatened by total destruction in the event of any major turmoil or faced with the possibility of being at the mercy of an agreement made over its head by the superpowers.

In response to this mediocre outlook, can Europe contribute to the building of a truly polycentric world in every sense of the term, that is to say, a world respectful of different social and economic paths of development? Such a new international order could open the way in Europe itself to social advances impossible to achieve within the strict logic of "competitiveness" alone. In other words, it could permit the beginning of breakthroughs in the direction of the extension of non-market social spaces, the only path for socialist progress in the West. Relaxed East-West relations in Europe, replacing the strategy of tension via the arms race and the dangerous illusion of succeeding by this means in detaching Eastern Europe from the Soviet Union, would also favor the democratic socialist progress that Gorbachev seems to desire. Different North-South relationships could thus be promoted in a context conducive to the objectively necessary popular national transition in the Third World. This option of "European nonalignment"—the form of "delinking" appropriate to this region of the world—is the only means for checking an otherwise almost inevitable decline.[13] Here I mean by decline the renunciation of a mobilizing and credible progressive social project in favor of day-to-day "adjustment" to outside forces.

Eurocentrism has led the world into a serious impasse. If the West remains locked into the positions that it has dictated in every area of political relationships, most notably North-South and East-West relationships, the risks of violent conflicts and of

[13]See CEDETIM, *Le Non-alignement européen* (Paris: La Découverte).

an increase in brutal racist positions will grow. A more humane future—one that is universalist and respectful of all—is not an ineluctable necessity, destined to impose itself; it is only an objectively necessary possibility, for which one must strive. The option remains true and thus necessarily socialist universalism or Eurocentric capitalist barbarism. To undertake the necessary struggle, the Left must be actively aware of these fundamental questions.

Socialism is at the end of this long tunnel. Let us understand by this a society that has resolved the legacy of the unequal development inherent to capitalism and has simultaneously given all human beings on the planet a better mastery of their social development. This society will be superior to ours on all levels only if it is worldwide, and only if it establishes a genuine universalism, based on contributions of everyone, Westerners as well as those whose historical course has been different. It is obvious that the long road which remains to be traveled in order to realize this goal prohibits the formulation of "definitive" judgments on the strategies and the stages to be passed, and that political and ideological confrontations like those that opposed "revolutionaries" and "social democrats" in their time, are nothing more than the vicissitudes of this long struggle. It is clear that the nature of this human society cannot be predicted.

The future is still open. It is still to be lived.